Seasons and Saints for the Christian Year

Resources for celebrating
the three-year lectionary
with children

Nicola and Stuart Currie

The National Society
A Christian Voice in Education

a co-publication with
Church House Publishing

National Society/Church House Publishing
Church House
Great Smith Street
London
SW1P 3NZ

ISBN 07151 4901 6

First published in 1998 by The National Society/Church House Publishing.

Cover design by Julian Smith
Printed by The Cromwell Press, Trowbridge, Wiltshire

Contents

Acknowledgements

The publisher gratefully acknowledges permission to reproduce copyright material in this book. Every effort has been made to trace and contact copyright holders. If there are any inadvertent omissions we apologise to those concerned and will ensure that a suitable acknowledgement is made at the next reprint.

The Central Board of Finance of the Church of England: Prayer from *Patterns for Worship* (Church House Publishing, 1995) (p. 10); prayer from *The Christian Year: Calendar, Lectionary and Collects* (Church House Publishing, 1997) (pp. 23, 96)

The *Church Times*: Chapters on St Valentine (pp. 17-19), Janani Luwum (pp. 20-23) and William Wilberforce (pp. 67-71)

General Synod of the Anglican Church of Canada: Excerpt from *The Book of Alternative Services of the Anglican Church of Canada.* Copyright © 1985 by the General Synod of the Anglican Church of Canada. Published by the Anglican Book Centre. Used with permission (p. 69).

Junior Church of St Stephen's, Worcester: Their help in testing many of the activities

McCrimmon Publishing: 'When Israel was in Egypt's land' (traditional Spiritual) from *Celebration Hymnal for Everyone*, vol. 2 (full music edn, 1995) (p. 70)

Morehouse Publishing: 'I sing a song of the saints', text © Lesbia Scott 1929, melody © John Henry Hopkins ('Grand Isle') 1940 (p. 98)

Robin Sharples, Children's Work Officer, Worcester Diocese: Contributions to the cross ideas for Good Friday (pp. 34-9)

SPCK: Circle prayer from David Adams, *The Edge of Glory*, SPCK, 1985 (p. 85)

Walton Music Corporation: 'Thuma mina', words and music copyright © 1984 Utryck. Used by permission (p. 57)

Unless otherwise indicated, the Bible quotations are taken from the Revised Standard Version (RSV), copyright © 1971 and 1952 by the Division of Christian Education of the National Council of the Churches of Christ in the USA. Additional quotations are taken from the New Revised Standard Version Bible (NRSV), copyright © 1989 by the Division of Christian Education of the National Council of the Churches of Christ in the USA, and the Good News Bible (GNB) published by the Bible Societies and HarperCollins Publishers, © American Bible Society 1994. Used by permission. All rights reserved.

Illustrations

AKG London: Hans Memling, *St Benedict* from the Uffizi Gallery, Florence (p. 64)

Bridgeman Art Library, London/New York: *Return of the Prodigal Son* by Harmensz van Rijn Rembrandt (1606-69), Hermitage, St Petersburg (p. 87)

Trustees of the British Museum: Water Newton plaque (p. 62)

Cafod: Oscar Romero, © Joe Fish (p. 28)

The Catholic Truth Society: Photograph from *Twentieth Century Martyrs: Maximilian Kolbe* (Incorporated Catholic Truth Society, 1997) (p.72)

Church Missionary Society: Archbishop Janani Luwum (p. 20) and William Wilberforce (p. 67)

Estudio Corte Real, Maputo: Bernard Mizeki. Kindly provided by the Bishop of Lobombo (p. 53)

Jane Gray: The Calling of Andrew, Pitminster Church, Somerset. Designed and made in 1989 by Jane Gray. Photograph by Peter Musgrave (p. 100)

Historic Scotland: Whithorn crosses (p. 83)

Hulton Getty Picture Collection: Gladys Aylward (p. 7)

Mary Evans Picture Library: St Valentine (p. 17), St Bede (p. 50), the Blessed Virgin Mary (p. 80) and Alfred the Great (p. 91)

The National Society (Church of England) for Promoting Religious Education: (p. 24)

Pam Pott: Celtic interlocking circles (p. 86)

Salvation Army Heritage Centre and the Salvation Army: photographs (pp. 75, 76 and 77).

G. Sayer (Oxfam): Photograph of Makonde sculpture (p. 22)

Robin Sharples, the Children's Work Officer for Worcester Diocese: the photograph of the display of Good Friday posters and lanterns (p. 34)

Swedish Tourist Board: photograph of the Lucy Queen (p. 1)

The Board of Trinity College Dublin: *St Alban and Priest* from Matthew Paris, *The Life of St Alban* (p. 58)

Jon Williams: photograph of the Bernard Mizeki shrine (p. 54)

Introduction

Seasons and Saints for the Christian Year is an action-packed practical resource book on Christian festivals and saints' days. It is designed for all who work with children under eleven in church groups, schools, midweek clubs, family services and for those one-off events.

There are 24 chapters which provide ideas for celebrating the Christian faith throughout the year. They are based on the new Church of England lectionary of saints' days and festivals. Two other commemorations – St Valentine and Gladys Alyward – are included because they often feature in school activities.

From Christmas eggs to Easter crackers this is a fun-based activity book. Each chapter provides background historical information, biblical starting points, discussion questions, worship ideas and suggestions for practical activities. The emphasis is on learning through experience: this is a hands-on craft-based approach.

The lives of saints including modern heroes of the faith have inspired and encouraged many people in their faith journey. This book takes an aspect of the faith and life of a saint and relates it to the life experience of a child.

How to use this book

This is a book to dip into. Each chapter is self-contained and can be used on a one-off basis. Some suggestions will need to be adapted to suit your local conditions. Others will need advance planning and where this is the case it is indicated in the introduction to the activity. We have assumed that the standard session will last half an hour.

The 1989 Children Act specifies the amount of care and supervision necessary for children, particularly the under-eights. If the event you are planning will last over two hours and involves the care of the under-eights then you must inform the local authority Social Services department. The Children Act requires you to inform the department in advance and you will need to register with them if your two-hour sessions become frequent events. Each diocese in the Church of England has Child Protection guidelines and it is therefore assumed that children's workers use these guidelines in their work with children in the Church.

Introduction to saints

It is very common practice in the Church to use a word in both a specific and a general sense. 'Priest' is applied specifically to those who have been ordained in the Church, yet this is in no sense contradictory to the notion of the 'priesthood of all believers' (1 Peter 2.9). If people were asked to name 'the disciples', twelve candidates would head the list, but the list includes all Christian people. Some have distinguished themselves as evangelists, yet all Christians are to spread the 'good news', the *ev-angel*. So likewise 'saints': St Paul uses the term to apply to all who have been baptized; many since have adopted this usage. At the same time the term has been given a technical definition: those who have been formally canonized. In the West only the Roman Catholic Church has a formal procedure for canonization, administered by the Congregation for the Causes of Saints. Among the tokens of honour conferred by canonization are public recognition, commemoration of a festival day and the possibility of having a church dedicated to God in memory of the saint. Those faithful departed who have received such recognition are known by the title 'Saint' plus their name.

In all instances mentioned – priest, disciple, evangelist, saint – the common theme is that certain people embody in their lives a particular attribute to which all Christians should aspire. 'Saint' means 'holy', and in the quest for holiness many saints (small s) have been inspired, encouraged and strengthened by the Saints (capital S).

The Church of England is part of the one, holy, catholic and apostolic church; it has no means of canonization. English Anglicans vary in their attitude to the cult of the saints, but the compilers of the new calendar have recognized that those who follow Christ encourage one another and are encouraged by examples of holiness. The calendar therefore allows for the commemoration of a number of Christians – mainly from the modern era – who have not been formally proclaimed 'Saint', but who are felt to have high exemplary value. Those individuals who are included in the calendar are not to be understood as the 'VIPs' of the faith, but as those whose lives point to Christ and whose examples inspire devotion to him.

St Lucy

Lighting up Advent

Each village in Sweden elects a Lucy Queen for St Lucy's day Photo: *Swedish Tourist Board*

The information we have about St Lucy seems to consist of one part fact and ten parts legend. Some regard this as unfortunate, but given the content of the legends, it is perhaps just as well that this should be so – at least for those who work with children. They need not, for instance, be taught that her eyes were torn out (possibly by herself) and then miraculously restored (though this knowledge is useful in identifying her in art, where she commonly holds her eyes on a cushion). They can also be spared the story of her punishment for refusing to marry a pagan suitor: she was to be put into a brothel and forced to become a prostitute, but, again by a miracle, she was made immovable so the guards could not take her away. Having thus failed, the judge then ordered her to be burned, but this too did not work. Eventually a sword was run through her throat and she died. Without the gory detail, all that remains is the story of a Sicilian girl, probably of noble birth, who gave gifts to the poor and who refused to marry because she had promised herself to Christ alone, as do nuns today. But because she lived at a time when the Roman Emperor was attacking the Church, her commitment to Christ exposed her to danger. In the persecution of AD 303–4 she paid the ultimate price and died for her faith. Thus she is numbered among the most celebrated virgin martyrs.

Themes

From the gruesome details above it will be obvious why Lucy is the patron of those who suffer from eye disease and throat infections, as well as glaziers and cutlers. Fortunately her name alone, derived from the Latin *lux*, light, adequately explains the more important of these patronages. Her feast day, 13 December, also makes her the light-bearer, and in Scandinavia her day is kept as a 'little Yule' anticipating the arrival of the light of the world at Christmas. Each village in Sweden elects a Lucy Queen who dresses in white with a head-dress including candles and takes cakes and sweets to the children. These activities explore the association of **light** and **gifts.**

TIMING

The candle-holders will take part of two sessions, as the clay will need to dry out in order to be painted. The chocolate candle cake will take one session.

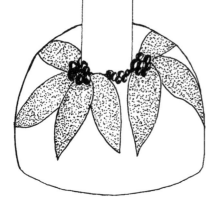

Activity ideas
Candle-holders – for all ages

Talk with the group about how St Lucy is celebrated in Sweden. Explain the importance of the theme of light in Advent, as Christians prepare for the 'Light of Christ' at Christmas. They can then make these simple candle-holders. When the holders are completed they can be used with candles in one of the Christmas services or celebrations.

You will need

a pack of modelling clay – the type that dries out and can be painted

small candles

table coverings and aprons

rolling pins and cutters

paints – 'Deco gloss' works well

METHOD

- Give each child a small lump of clay and ask them to work it into a small ball.
- They then need to flatten it slightly and carefully push in the candle into the centre, making sure that the candle does not go all the way through the ball.
- The candle is taken out.
- Using small pieces of clay they can model different shapes and press them around the candle ring.
- The ring is left to dry for a week.
- The following week the children can paint their candle rings.

Chocolate candle cake gifts – for all ages

Talk with the group about the importance of gift-giving at Christmas. Explain that God gave the gift of his Son at Christmas, Christians therefore remember this through giving gifts to each other. This no-bake chocolate cake can be cut up at the end of the session and given as gifts to the friends and relatives of the children.

This recipe will make one tray of the cake. You might want to divide the group up into twos or threes and each small group make one tray.

METHOD

- Break up 400 g of the chocolate and cut up the butter and place in a bowl.
- An adult should melt the chocolate with the butter in a microwave according to the manufacturer's instructions or in the bowl over a pan of hot water.
- Grease the baking tray.
- Place the broken biscuits, cereal and dried fruit into the chocolate mixture and stir in well.
- Put this mixture into the greased tray and press down so that you have a flat surface.
- Prepare the chocolate topping by melting the 200 g of chocolate in the same way as before.
- Cover the cake with the topping and allow to cool slightly.
- Empty the tube of the chocolate beans on to the table and separate the colours.
- Use the 'hot' colours – red, orange and yellow – to make a flame shape on the table.
- Use the remaining colours to make the candle shape.
- Transfer the two shapes on to the topping on the cake so that you have a candle cake.
- The cake can be cut up and distributed as gifts.

For one large tray of cake you will need

a cooking hob or microwave

a saucepan

a heatproof bowl that fits into the top of the saucepan

two bowls

a non-stick baking tray

400 g chocolate for the cake

200 g chocolate for the topping

250 g butter or hard margarine

100 g toasted rice cereal (Rice Krispies *or* similar)

200 g dried fruit

200 g broken biscuits

a large tube of candy-coated chocolate beans

table coverings and aprons

cooking utensils

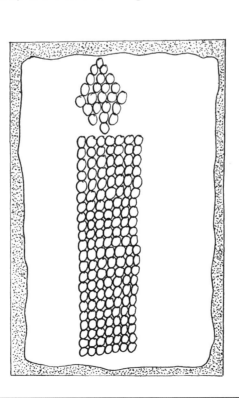

Christmas

A
t Christmas it is of course the story that commands attention – and rightly so. Matthew and Luke record different aspects of this story, and both recognize that it holds truths which cannot be expressed in any other way. It is therefore vital to continue the tradition of introducing children to the story, of offering it to them as a gift complete in itself. Those who work with children will make that introduction real through nativity plays, tableaux and narrative. At the same time it is important to encourage some reflection on the meaning of the story, to allow children to encounter some of the inexhaustible truths conveyed by the opening chapters of Matthew and Luke. Any selection will of course be partial: the aim is to initiate a process of exploration, not to offer a definitive, once-for-all interpretation – the mystery of the incarnation is too rich and too profound for a such a thing to be possible.

Activity ideas

THEMES

'Glory to God in the highest heaven, and on earth peace among those whom he favours' (Luke 2.14 NRSV). The message of the angels is of universal peace. Jesus is the longed-for Messiah whom Isaiah called 'Wonderful Counsellor, Mighty God, Everlasting Father, Prince of Peace' (Isaiah 9.6). Jesus expresses this universality in personal terms: 'Whoever does the will of God is my brother, and sister, and mother' (Mark 3.35). Christian faith holds that through the birth of the saviour of the world, all people are invited into the same relationship with God; and therefore all people can enjoy the same relationship with one another, as brothers and sisters belonging to the same **family**.

A constant theme of the nativity story is **fragility**, precariousness and risk. God through an angel visits a simple peasant girl and invites her to respond. Had she said 'No', God would presumably have sought another way. So he runs the risk of rejection. Mary is an unlikely candidate for God's purpose, and she is not even married. The journey to Bethlehem at an advanced stage of pregnancy was risky in the extreme. And giving birth in a smelly stable, with none of the hi-tech resources of the twentieth century available, was hardly less precarious. The story of Christ's birth shows us God in vulnerability, depending on human care and love.

The Christmas narrative is of course a very human story – we have all been through birth. But the evangelists are not only interested in its humanity: their interest is in what the story reveals about God.

The activities below explore the themes of **belonging** by adapting the Christmas tree as a family tree; the theme of **fragility** by making Christmas eggs – which have been deliberately 'stolen' from Easter to make the connection between the incarnation and the resurrection; and the theme of **revelation** through the card.

TIMING

Each activity can take part of one session.

You will need

some large sheets of card-board

paint and paint-brushes

table coverings and aprons

drawing materials

tinsel

sticky tape

portrait pictures of members of the congregation

gift ribbon

Christmas family tree – for all ages

Matthew's account of the first Christmas begins with the long family tree of Jesus' ancestors. Jesus was part of a larger family. He was born in Bethlehem because his family had to be registered in the place of their ancestors. Most children are familiar with family trees and the leader can talk with them about these and perhaps even show them a family tree. Children are less familiar with the concept that they are part of the Christian family. Christmas is an appropriate time to focus on the Christian family of the Church.

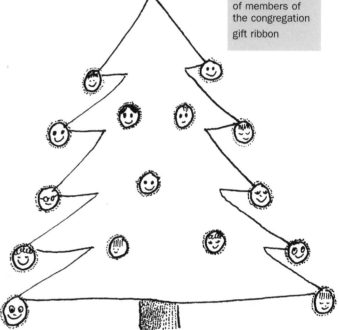

METHOD

- Make a large cardboard Christmas tree.
- Paint with green paint and dry.
- Cut out a series of card circles – the 'baubles' of the tree.
- Cut out the faces from the photographs to fit onto the 'bauble' shapes and glue together.
- Encircle the 'bauble' photograph with tinsel and secure with sticky tape.
- Attach a piece of gift ribbon to each 'bauble' and hang from the tree.

Christmas eggs – for older children

This simple Christmas tree decoration reminds the children that the infant Jesus was a small, fragile and vulnerable baby.

METHOD

- Prick each end of a cleaned egg with a pin so that there is a hole in both ends of the egg.
- Carefully prick the yolk and blow down the egg so that the contents fall into a bowl.
- Dry the egg on a piece of kitchen paper.
- Paint the figure of the baby Jesus wrapped in swaddling clothes on to the egg with the paints.

You will need

a large egg for each child with some to spare

a pin

kitchen paper

a bowl

table coverings and aprons

'Deco gloss' paints or poster paints

paint brushes

gift ribbon

Copydex glue

- Once the egg is dry a loop of gift ribbon can be attached to the top of the egg with Copydex.
- When the glue has dried the egg can be hung from a tree.

A stable door card – for all ages

This simple card can be made in between rehearsals for the annual nativity play.

METHOD

- Find the centre of the card and fold down each edge to the centre as shown.
- Cut the top of the card as shown.
- On the front of the card ask the children to draw the stable doors.
- They can open the cards and draw angels or animals on the inside of the stable doors and a crib scene in the centre of the card (see page 4).

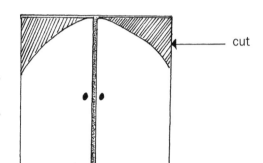

cut

You will need

a piece of A4 white card for each child.

brown wax crayons

drawing materials

scissors

Gladys Aylward

A missionary in China

Gladys Aylward Photo: *Hulton Getty Picture Collection*

Few women missionaries have caught the public's imagination as much as Gladys Aylward. Her life, now recorded in many books and a feature film, reveals a woman of extraordinary courage, determination and compassion. Her popularity survives her death in 1970 and her story continues to be told to new generations of schoolchildren.

Gladys Aylward did not go to China through the usual missionary channels. She was rejected by the China Inland Mission for missionary service because it was believed that she was not capable of learning the languages needed. Born in 1902, Gladys was brought up in London. She left school at 14 as she says of herself, 'as far as I can find out, having passed one exam'. Her first job was with Marks & Spencer, then the Penny Bazaar, after which she worked as a parlour maid. Gladys was convinced that God was asking her to work in China. She sold many of her personal belongings and did extra work to pay for her fare to China. In October 1930 she had finally saved enough to buy a third-class ticket on the Trans-Siberian Railway. Thus began an extraordinary train journey which took her through war-torn Russia via Japan to China.

Gladys Aylward's destination was Yangcheng in South Shansi in North China where she had promised to join an elderly Scottish missionary, Jeannie Lawson. The people who lived in the area had a hard life and before Jeannie Lawson's arrival knew nothing of the Christian story. The two women decided to open up an inn where travellers could rest. At first the travellers were afraid of the 'foreign devils' but gradually they came to enjoy listening to the stories of Jesus from the missionaries. The inn became the first church in the area. After Jeannie Lawson died Gladys was given the unusual job of 'foot inspector' by the local Mandarin. In those days the traditional Chinese custom was for girl babies to have their feet bound so that they would not grow. Small feet were considered beautiful. But the local Mandarin realized the pain and suffering caused by this custom and ruled that all feet should be unbound. This was a potentially unpopular decree, and Gladys Aylward, a foreigner, was chosen to enforce it. After initial doubts she realized that she could preach the gospel in the surrounding area while inspecting feet.

Throughout her life Gladys had an important ministry to children. She took a number of abandoned children into the inn. For many years she worked in the hill areas around Yangcheng. She learnt all the local languages and many local people became Christians. Because of the war between the Chinese and the Japanese, Gladys was forced to flee the area. She took more than a hundred children with her. The story of her epic journey with a hundred children across the mountains and the Yellow River to Sian has become legendary. Gladys became ill during the journey and spent a long time recuperating. In 1949 she returned to Britain. Later she went to Hong Kong and then Taiwan, as the political situation meant she could not get back into China. In Taiwan she opened a home for orphaned and abandoned babies. Gladys Aylward died on 2 January 1970 at the age of 61.

THEMES

The story of Gladys Aylward provides a rich source of material for work with children. Her friends, 'children' and writings survive her and so it is possible for the children's work leader to use recent material to show children the life of a modern 'saint' to whom they can relate. The particular themes explored in the activities are:

Readiness to do God's work – Gladys Aylward was ready to do whatever God wanted of her throughout her life.

Following the light of Christ – Gladys Aylward relied on Jesus to illuminate her way.

Walking in Christ's footsteps – for Gladys Aylward the Christian journey through life was often literally a journey: her journey to China; her journeys through the mountain villages as a foot inspector; her journey across China with the children and then her journeys to Britain, Hong Kong and Taiwan.

Courage – throughout her life Gladys Aylward showed remarkable courage and determination.

TIMING

The footsteps frieze and the lanterns will take most of one session. The other activities can be combined to form a session.

Activity ideas

Gladys Aylward was always **ready to do God's will.** She was determined to work in China for God despite all the things which could have prevented her. Through her prayers and reading of the Bible she continued to ask God what he wanted her to do. She writes: 'I discovered that through faith one could do anything; God kept his promise and it needed me to take him at his word and all would be well.' This activity explores the idea of being ready for God.

Packing a suitcase – for younger children

Talk with the children about what their families do when they need to go away on holiday. Discuss with them the type of things that they would pack into a case. Then ask them to pretend that they are Gladys Aylward. What would she have taken on her long train journey to China?

Then tell them what Gladys Aylward did take on the journey: clothes, tins of corned beef, fish and baked beans, biscuits, soda cakes, meat cubes, coffee essence, tea and hard-boiled eggs. She also had a saucepan, a kettle, a spirit stove and a Bible. With these items and a small amount of money she left everything she knew to go into the unknown.

Explain to the group that Gladys Aylward not only got ready for her long and difficult journey to China but she also made sure that she was always ready to listen to God. Discuss with the group how people can listen to God. Explain that Gladys Aylward listened to God by reading her Bible and saying her prayers. The children can then make a copy of Gladys Aylward's bag.

You will need

a set of card cut-out suitcases

drawing materials

scissors

METHOD

- Fold a piece of card in half and cut out a suitcase shape as indicated in the illustration.
- Give each child a card suitcase.
- Ask them to open their suitcases and on one side draw all the things that Gladys Aylward took with her to China apart from the Bible.

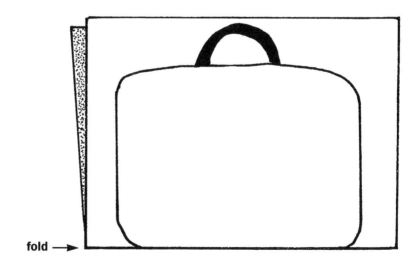

fold →

- Then ask the children to draw a picture of a Bible in the other side of the suitcase.

Chinese lanterns – for older children

Almighty God,
we thank you for the gift of your holy Word.
May it be a lantern to our feet,
a light to our paths,
and a strength to our lives.
Take us and use us
to love and serve
in the power of the Holy Spirit
and in the name of your Son,
Jesus Christ our Lord.

From *Patterns for Worship*, page 97

Throughout her life Gladys Aylward trusted in God. God was the only focus of her work and she relied on Jesus to illuminate her way. Discuss with the group the idea of 'the light of Christ'. What do they understand by this? Then say the prayer above with them. In what way can Jesus be a 'lantern to our feet?' or a 'light to our paths?' The group can then make these Chinese lanterns to remind them of the image.

METHOD

- Cut out two large circles on the hologram or shiny paper using a large plate to draw around.
- Fold each circle in half four times.
- Make deep cuts into the paper from the sides as shown (fig. a).
- Carefully open up the paper and flatten.
- Glue small circles of stiff card to the centre of each circle on the non-shiny side.
- When the card circles are dry thread a double thread of cotton through the centre of one of the circles and knot at both ends of the thread.
- Secure one knotted thread end on the card with a piece of sticky tape.
- On the non-shiny side of the other circle spot glue on every other fold as shown (fig. b).
- Press the threaded circle on the sticky circle and press hard.
- When the glue is dry carefully pull the lantern slits apart.
- Attach the other thread end to a pea stick or chopstick.
- Hang the lantern up (fig. c).

Fig. a

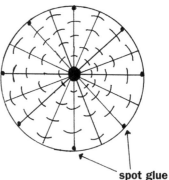

spot glue

Fig. b

Fig. c

You will need

pencils
a large plate
sheets of hologram or shiny paper
scissors
card
sticky tape
needle and thread
stick of glue
pea sticks or chopsticks

Gladys Aylward wrote: 'He will show you the path He wants you to tread. After the first step the rest is easy; you just keep going, knowing he is always in front leading.' Remind the group that Gladys Aylward promised to follow God. She promised to follow in the footsteps of Jesus. Ask them what people mean when they say: 'Are you going to follow in your father's/mother's footsteps?' What does to 'follow in the footsteps' of someone mean? Then explain that you are going to work out how people can **follow in the footsteps of Jesus.**

Footsteps frieze – for younger children

Discuss how Christians follow in the footsteps of Jesus. What was Jesus like? Make a list of all the attributes they give Jesus – loving, kind, etc. Then sing the hymn 'O Jesus, I Have Promised'. Discuss the verse beginning 'O, let me see thy foot marks and in them plant my own'.

METHOD

- On each of the left paper feet write one attribute of Jesus.
- Discuss each attribute in turn and ask the children to think of a person in their group who has shown this characteristic during the past week. Elicit from the group some of Jesus' attributes such as loving, caring, healing, etc. and at least one instance of that attribute in someone in the group.
- When a child is named as having shown care, love, etc. they should draw around their own right foot on a piece of paper and write their name on it and decorate it.
- The children's cut-out feet can then be glued on to the right foot of 'Jesus' opposite the appropriate attribute on the left foot.
- The completed feet can be mounted on a large sheet of paper as a frieze and headed 'Let me see thy foot marks and in them plant my own'.

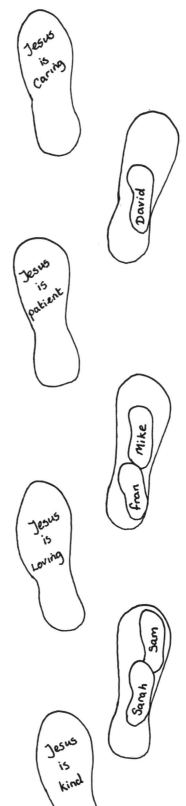

Medallions – for younger children

Gladys Aylward left her home, family and friends to set off for China with very few resources. In her work with the travellers, in speaking with the mighty Mandarin, in quelling a prison riot, and later in her journey across China with the children, she showed exceptional courage. Throughout she trusted in God.

Tell the group the story of how Gladys Aylward quelled a prison riot based on this outline. After she had lived for some time in Yangcheng, Gladys Aylward was summoned to break up a riot in the local men's prison. She protested to the Governor that she was not the person to break up a fight between murderers, bandits, and thieves but the Governor told her that the soldiers were too afraid to do it. When Gladys protested that the rioters might kill her, the Governor replied: 'But how can they kill you? You tell everybody that you have come here because you have the living God inside you . . . If you preach the truth, if your God protects you from harm, then you can stop this riot.' Gladys realized that if she did not go into the prison many local people would not believe in her God. So she asked for God's strength and went into the prison. Just as a prisoner was about to kill another with a large axe Gladys shouted for him to give it to her. She then ordered the stunned prisoners to form a line and asked them what their grievance was that led to the fighting. She learnt about the appalling conditions in the prison and saw many of them for herself. She promised to help to improve the life of the prisoners and she kept her promise.

Discuss with the group people they know who have been courageous. In our society people who are courageous or show bravery are often rewarded by being given a medal or an award in recognition of their service. Gladys Aylward was recognized later in her life as a brave and courageous woman but for her the only worthwhile reward was having faith. The group can make these bravery medallions and either put in Gladys Aylward's name or their own name.

You will need

ribbon
discs of card
wax crayons
blunt pencils
scissors
sticky tape

METHOD

- Give each child a card disc.
- Ask them to cover one side of the card in yellow or orange wax crayon.
- They should then choose a dark-coloured wax crayon and colour over the layer of yellow or orange.
- They can then carefully scratch out a cross shape in the centre of the disc and the name 'Gladys' or their own name using a blunt pencil.
- They can then attach a loop of ribbon to the disc with a piece of sticky tape to make a medallion.

Remind the group that sometimes Christians are called to be brave for Jesus.

Epiphany

An Epiphany party

Photo:
*Nicola
Currie*

After all the Christingles, crib services and nativity plays, the feast of the Epiphany is often overlooked. The great arrival of the wise men from the east to visit Jesus is usually remembered in Advent during a nativity play and then forgotten about for another year. One way of ensuring that Epiphany is put back on the children's liturgical map is to have an Epiphany party. The advantage of an Epiphany party is that it begins the term or new year with a celebration.

THEMES

There are many themes in the Epiphany narrative (Matthew 2) which can be explored through a series of party games or during a lesson. Those explored in this material include:

Journey – the journey of Mary and Joseph to Bethlehem and then to Egypt and the journey of the wise men. Each journey had a purpose and would have involved careful preparation and some danger.

Gifts – 'Then, opening their treasures, they offered him gifts, gold and frankincense and myrrh' (Matthew 2.11). The wise men brought gifts fit for a king.

Immediately after Christmas the gift theme is a good one to explore with children. A session before the party could focus on the gift theme.

TIMING

It is possible to use some of this material in a teaching session before a party. The party ideas followed by the tea will take about two hours.

Teaching session

Explore the theme of gifts with the group. Ask the children what gifts they received for Christmas and why. What would they have bought a newborn baby? Then ask them to explain the gifts the wise men brought. Use the material on page 16 to explain the possible significance of the gifts. The children can then make the cut-out stars, colour in the cardboard drawing of a camel and make a wise man's hat.

Party ideas

ORGANIZE BEFOREHAND:

- plenty of adults to help supervise;
- invitations to the party to send to the children in advance of Christmas telling them the time and place of the party and asking them to dress up as a wise man;
- a set of sticky labels (enough to give each child a label) marked with the initials C, M, or B.

Preparation

The party room and food and drink will need to be prepared before the children arrive. Set up all the games in different parts of the room leaving plenty of space for the first game. Explain to the helpers that the party will be divided into three parts: games to do with the journey the wise men made, games on the gifts they brought and finally the stable party meal. Make sure there is a sticky label marked C, M, or B for each party-goer.

On the children's arrival

The party-goers are divided into three teams, the M team, the B team and the C team – Melchior, Balthazar and Caspar, some of the names traditionally given the Magi or wise men. As each 'wise man' arrives a sticky letter label can be stuck on their backs. While the children are assembling they can find out who else is in their team.

Once assembled the teams can play the first warm-up game, 'Cross the Euphrates', and then take it in turns to do each of the following games rotating between the three games on each theme.

Explain to the children that they are going to take part in a long journey like the one the Magi or wise men would have taken to visit Jesus in Bethlehem. But their journey will be fun and a series of party games. It is unclear who the wise men were or where they came from. It is likely that their journey involved crossing a river – perhaps it was the River Euphrates. The first adventure of

You will need

For crossing the Euphrates

chalk
a cleared space

For the camel game

a large piece of card with a camel shape on, drawing pins, sticky labels, pencils and a blindfold.

For the journey checklist

a trayful of about twenty objects needed for a desert journey – torch, map, food, money, compass, and a picture of a tent, clothes, waterproof, etc.

For the star game

gold card or paper cut into star shapes. On each star write an 'action' for the group to do, e.g. whistle a carol without laughing, hop around the room, etc. In advance of the event hide the stars around the room.

For gold caskets

three bags of gold chocolate coins, three boxes to throw the coins into.

For 'Find the frankincense'

empty yogurt pots each containing a cotton wool ball that has been impregnated with a smell, e.g. garlic, coffee, furniture polish, perfume. One cotton wool ball needs to be impregnated with oil of frankincense (available at some chemists). If frankincense oil is not available use incense. Label each pot a,b,c, etc.

For myrrh boxes

flat biscuits, prepared icing, small coloured sweets, table covers, and knives (or plain cake boxes and felt-tip pens)

party food and drink

their journey is to cross the mighty River Euphrates by all getting into a canoe. After that the wise men have to get a camel, prepare to cross a desert and follow the star which is not always easy to see. Then they have to find the gifts they will take to Jesus.

Crossing the Euphrates

In advance of the session draw two chalk lines to represent the banks of the river on opposite sides of the room. Each team then has to assemble on one bank and sit in line with their backs to the opposite bank, and with their legs apart around the child in front, as if they were a boat. After a signal is given, the child at the front of the line has to run round to the back of the line and sit behind the back person. Then the child who is at the front has to do that again and so on, until slowly the team move across the river space.

Getting ready for the journey

Collect a camel

This is a variation on 'pin the tail on the donkey'. Each child is given a small sticky label with their initials on. The child who manages to get their label in the correct position on the saddle of the pre-drawn camel while blindfolded wins.

Journey checklist

This is a version of 'Kim's Game'. Once the children have identified the objects on the tray which are needed for a desert journey, the leader has to secretly take one off or add a new object to the tray. The children have to identify which object is missing or has been added.

Follow the star

Before the session the leaders need to have hidden the 'action' stars; ask the children to find the stars and to do the actions.

Preparing the gifts

Gold caskets

Explain to the children that gold has always been a precious metal and an appropriate gift for a king to symbolize that he is prosperous and rich (Psalm 72.15; Isaiah 60.6). Jesus was not a rich man but he was a special type of king and the wise men brought him a gift fit for a king. Arrange a box some distance from where the children are standing. Give each child a golden chocolate coin and get them to throw it into the box. Once all the coins have been thrown in, the box of gold is ready for the wise men to take to the stable party.

Find the frankincense

Explain that frankincense is a gum obtained from the frankincense tree which grows in the Middle East. Frankincense was used in Old Testament times in sacrifice. It is a precious and sweet-smelling perfume often used to make incense. The children have to identify each of the smells in the yogurt pots. Which is the frankincense?

Myrrh boxes

Explain that myrrh is also from the resin of the gum tree and has been used as a medicine. It was used in anointing and in burial customs. In the Old Testament kings were consecrated for their high office by having oil poured on their heads. Traditionally this gift of myrrh was believed to show that the wise men recognized Jesus' kingship and perhaps knew he was to die.

Myrrh has always been very precious and would have been carried in highly decorated boxes in Jesus' day. The children can make their own decorated boxes by decorating a flat biscuit with icing and sweets. Alternatively the children can decorate plain cake boxes with felt-tip pen drawings. These boxes can then be used as a type of lunch box and 'doggy bag' for the party food.

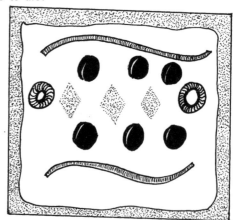

Stable party

Once the games are over the children can all have their tea. If you want to continue the thematic idea you could serve some Middle Eastern food including dates, figs, tangerines, pomegranates, almond biscuits and halva.

St Valentine

More than pink hearts and Cupid's darts

St Valentine.
*Anon. painting
on glass*
Photo: *Mary
Evans Picture
Library*

Who was St Valentine? No-one is really quite sure. His festival is rarely observed today in the Church so he is not exactly in the first division of saints. Nevertheless his popularity survives undiminished. Many children keep St Valentine's day on 14 February and there is still room for the resourceful teacher to get beyond the pink hearts and Cupids.

St Valentine is possibly an amalgamation of two people. The first St Valentine was probably a Roman priest martyred on the Flaminian Way during the reign of the Emperor Claudius (*c.* AD 269). According to legend Valentine looked after persecuted Christians, he became a convert, was persecuted himself and was clubbed to death. The second Valentine might have been the Bishop of Terni who was taken to Rome and martyred. Unfortunately, the accounts of both martyrs are thought to be unreliable.

The customs attached to St Valentine's day may derive from the pagan Roman festival of Lupercalia in mid-February. Lupercalia celebrated new life and fertility. It was the day for young men to select a woman of their choice. It may also be that St Valentine's day is associated with the first stirrings of spring when birds traditionally choose their mates. This is referred to by both Chaucer and Shakespeare.

THEMES

These activities explore the themes of **Christian love** and **affection**.

TIMING

The frieze and basket-making can each take one session. The cookery will need careful preparation to fit into one session. If time is limited then the biscuit dough can be made in advance.

Activity ideas
An agape collage – for older children

Explain to the group that in the Bible there are a number of different Greek words for the English word 'love'. The Greek word 'agape' in the New Testament means that special love followers of Jesus have and which they are called upon to show to their friends and enemies; the self-giving love that considers first the needs of others. Jesus' life and death epitomize this love. St Valentine the martyr also showed it when he helped persecuted Christians and gave his life for his beliefs.

Take a selection of magazines, charity newsletters, newspapers, etc. into the group. Ask the children to find pictures which illustrate the special sort of Christian love – agape. Discuss the pictures with the group and help them to cut them out and mount them on a collage.

> **You will need**
>
> a selection of magazines and newspapers
>
> a roll of plain paper
>
> scissors
>
> glue and spreaders

Valentine hearts

One of the many legends surrounding St Valentine is that he fell in love with his gaoler's daughter, and when he went to be executed he left a note for her signed 'Your Valentine'. That may not sound a likely story, but it would explain the origin of some of the Valentine's day customs of cards, letters, hearts and gifts. While children might not have a Valentine, they can make these heart-shaped baskets and biscuits to give to a friend.

> **You will need**
>
> sheets of card
>
> scissors
>
> colouring materials
>
> glue
>
> sweets

A simple basket – for younger children

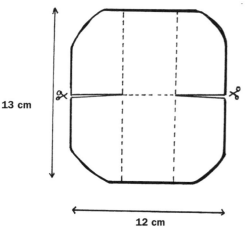

13 cm

12 cm

Fig. a

METHOD
- Cut out a sheet of card 13 cm x 12 cm.
- Mark up the sheet as shown in figure a and cut out.
- Cut off the corners to make rounded edges as shown.
- Colour and decorate the card on one side.
- Cut along the solid lines as shown.
- Fold the card into three along the two long dotted lines.
- Open out and then fold along the centre line.
- Fold the card to make a basket as shown in figure b and glue into position.
- Attach a strip of paper to make a handle as shown in figure c.
- Fill with sweets.

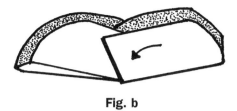

Fig. b

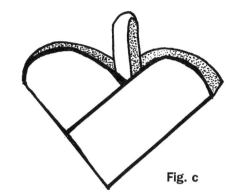

Fig. c

Sweetheart biscuits – for older children

This recipe makes about sixteen large transparent heart-centred biscuits and sixteen small heart-shaped biscuits. The small biscuits are made from the centres of the larger ones. The larger biscuits are difficult to make with smaller children and so they can decorate the smaller biscuits while the older children put sweet centres into theirs. The adult helpers should crush the sweets and supervise the cooking of the biscuits in the oven.

METHOD

- Set the oven at 170°C.
- Line the baking trays with silicone paper.
- Put the sweets into a double layer of plastic bags and secure. Gently hammer them to crush the sweets. The children can then prepare the rest of the ingredients.
- Mix together the flour, sugar and margarine/butter.
- Add the eggs to make a stiff dough.
- Knead the dough and form into a large ball.
- Carefully roll out the dough on a floured board to a thickness of 0.75 cm.
- Use a heart-shaped cutter (about 5 cm across) to cut a heart and leave the cutter in the dough.
- Around this cutter cut out a larger sized heart about 10 cm in height.
- Using a fish slice carefully lift the whole heart including the cutter on to the silicone paper.
- Take out the centre heart and place on the baking sheet. Younger children can decorate these smaller hearts by pushing fork shapes into the dough.
- In the heart centre of the larger biscuits carefully put a layer of crushed sweets.
- Using the straw mark a hole at the top centre of the biscuits so that the ribbon can be attached later.
- Cook all the biscuits for about 15–20 minutes until golden.
- Carefully remove the biscuits from the oven and leave until cold. The syrup in the centre is extremely hot and needs to be left to set and cool.
- Once cold the biscuits can be tied up with ribbons and offered to friends and family by the children.

You will need

400 g plain flour

200 g sugar

200 g margarine or butter

two eggs beaten together

three tubes of red boiled sweets

heart-shaped cutter

hammer and two thick plastic bags

knives and forks

fish slice

silicone paper/baking parchment

baking trays

rolling pin

a straw

gift ribbon

Janani Luwum

A modern martyr in Uganda

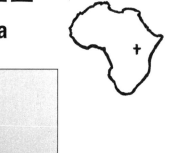

*Archbishop
Janani Luwum
Photo: Church
Missionary Society*

Perhaps the most famous modern martyr of the African Church is Archbishop Janani Luwum. The Church in Uganda commemorates his martyrdom on 16 February and the Church of England on 17 February.

Janani Luwum was born in 1922 at Mucwini in East Acholi in Uganda. His father was a convert to Christianity. Janani was a teacher before he started his ordination training. He was made deacon in 1955 and quickly became established as a Church leader and teacher. In 1969 he was consecrated Bishop of Northern Uganda.

In 1974 he became Archbishop of Uganda, Rwanda, Burundi and Boga-Zaire.

Three years previously Colonel Idi Amin had overthrown the elected government of Uganda and established a military dictatorship. Amin's regime became infamous around the world. The Church was outspoken in expressing its concern about violations of human rights and this cost it dear.

Tension between Church and state worsened in 1976. Religious leaders, including Archbishop Luwum, met to discuss the breakdown of law and order in Ankole. The government accused religious organizations of using their places of worship to plot against the government. President Amin reprimanded Archbishop Luwum.

On 5 February 1977 the Archbishop's house was raided by soldiers who said they had been ordered to look for arms. On 8 February the Archbishop and nearly all the Ugandan bishops met and drafted a letter of protest to the President and asked to see him. A week later, on 16 February, the Archbishop and six bishops were publicly arraigned in a show trial and were accused of smuggling arms. Archbishop Luwum was not allowed to reply, but shook his head in denial. The Vice-President concluded by asking the crowd: 'What shall we do with these traitors?' The soldiers replied, 'Kill them now.' The Archbishop was separated from his bishops and taken to see President Amin. As he was taken away Archbishop Luwum turned to his brother bishops and said: 'Do not be afraid. I see God's hand in this'.

The next morning it was announced that Archbishop Luwum had been killed in a car crash. The truth was that he had been shot because he had stood up to President Amin and his Government.

THEMES

People will often especially remember the death of a loved one on their birthday or the anniversary of their death. Christians remember the special holy people of the Church on their anniversary. This remembrance often combines four elements: the **retelling of the life**; recognizing the **communion of saints**; **thanking God** for the life; and **asking God that we learn from the example**. These four elements can form the basis of a number of activities or worship.

TIMING

The drama and prayer activity can combine to form one session. Each of the craft activities will take a session.

Activity ideas

These activity ideas can be adapted for teaching about any saint or martyr.

Act it out – for all ages

The story of Archbishop Janani Luwum is dramatic. The last few days of his life can be turned into a drama by children with players acting out Idi Amin, Archbishop Luwum and his wife Mary, soldiers, bishops, etc. Alternatively, the children can reproduce scenes from the last days of his life on a cereal-box TV.

METHOD

- Cut out the cereal box to make a TV.
- Mark out frames on the roll of paper to fit behind the screen.
- The children can then draw scenes from Archbishop Luwum's life on the frames.
- Thread the spoons through holes at the top of the TV box and attach each end of the roll of paper to the spoon handles with sticky tape.
- The children can then compose a commentary for their own TV news, winding on the film with the spoons.

The communion of saints – for all ages

Martyrs like Janani Luwum provide an example of how a Christian life can build up and strengthen the whole body of Christ. Uganda and Archbishop Luwum may seem far removed from the children's own experience but their Christian story is linked to those of Christians in Uganda. They are part of the same Christian community which is united in prayer to God.

One way to illustrate this inter-relatedness of the whole Christian community is by showing the children some Makonde art from Tanzania (see illustration). In these wooden sculptures each figure depends on another for its support but all are united in the whole sculpture.

The children can create their own simple model by linking paper cut-out models of people around a clear plastic bottle. Divide the children into groups of three and give each group a plastic bottle and drawing materials.

An example of Makonde sculpture Photo: Oxfam

METHOD

- Ask them to draw a simple outline of themselves with outstretched hands and to cut this out and colour it in. The drawings need to be about 8 cm high.
- Ask the children to think of the people who have helped them in their faith. Perhaps it is their parents, their godparents, a teacher, a church person, a brother or sister.
- Ask them to draw pictures of people who have helped them in their faith, again with outstretched hands.
- Finally ask them to draw a picture of Jesus, a saint or a famous Christian leader who has inspired them. These figures should also have outstretched hands.
- When the children have cut out all their paper people they can paste them on to the bottle, linking the figures' hands.
- The completed bottle can remind them that they are not alone on the Christian journey but part of a larger body of Christians and the Church.

Thanksgiving prayer – for all ages

Thanking God in prayer

God of truth,
whose servant Janani Luwum walked in the light,
and in his death defied the powers of darkness:
free us from fear of those who kill the body,
that we too may walk as children of light,
through him who overcame darkness
by the power of the cross,
Jesus Christ your Son our Lord,
who is alive and reigns with you,
in the unity of the Holy Spirit,
one God, now and for ever.

Collect for 17 February in
The Christian Year: Calendar, Lectionary and Collects

Read this collect to the children and then ask them to compose their own prayer which gives thanks to God for the brave witness of Janani Luwum. If there is time the children can be helped to put together their own simple service which includes a dramatic retelling of Archbishop Luwum's life and a time of prayer.

Mothering Sunday

Fourth Sunday of Lent

Photo:
*The
National
Society*

Mothering Sunday has many names and over the centuries it has had many faces. It is possible that the Church 'borrowed' an ancient Roman custom of honouring motherhood in spring with the feast of Matronalia. Mothering Sunday is also known as Refreshment Sunday, or Laetare Sunday. The name Laetare comes from the first Latin word of the traditional opening prayer of the Mass 'Laetare Jerusalem' – 'Rejoice Jerusalem'. It was the Sunday when the strict fasting rules of Lent were relaxed, refreshment was taken and people looked forward to Easter. Refreshment Sunday may also owe its name to the Gospel reading for the day in *The Book of Common Prayer*, which is the feeding of the five thousand.

At some point in the past two centuries the emphasis shifted from honouring Mother Church on Refreshment Sunday to honouring mothers. From the eighteenth century Mothering Sunday was a day when domestic servants were given time off to visit their own homes and mothers. Mother's Day is said to be an American invention which arrived in England with the American armed forces during the second World War. They brought their May customs of honouring their mothers with gifts of cards, flowers and sweets.

Today the festival continues to be adapted. The themes of mothering, caring and giving thanks remain and churches are often sensitive to the mothering everyone does in the home or community.

THEMES

The themes of **mothering**, **caring** and **giving thanks** are the traditional themes of Mothering Sunday. These activities explore the analogy of the motherhood of God through a simple Bible study and provide two craft activities so that children can express their thanks to their own mothers.

TIMING

The Bible study will take about ten minutes. The craft activities will need to be done in advance of Mothering Sunday and are designed to provide a card, and a vase for the traditional gift of flowers. The card can be done in one session by older children but younger children might need the cards prepared for them ready to colour in. The glass painting is designed only for patient older children and can be completed in one session. Younger children can decorate a glass vase with sticky collage materials.

Activity ideas

Motherhood and God – a Bible study for older children

In doing this Bible study the teacher and children's worker will need to be sensitive to the different family situations of the children.

For most children their first experience of love is from their parents. When adults talk about the love of God, the love that children know about is that given by those around them. Within this love of the family and community there is often the special affection and love the child receives from his or her mother. It is often the mother who provides the first food, warmth and affection. For centuries the Church has referred to God as father. Jesus himself referred to God as Abba (Daddy) but the analogy of motherhood is sometimes used to help express the unique love and compassion of God. Mothering Sunday is an appropriate time to explore this analogy with children.

Ask the children to say the Our Father. Then ask them to say the same prayer only beginning 'Our Mother'. Discuss with them how saying 'Our Mother, who art in heaven,' changes the prayer for them. What do they imagine when they say 'Our Father? In what ways do they think of God as Father? How is God like a father? What do they think when they say 'Our Mother, who art in heaven . . .'? In what ways is God like a mother?

Then help the children look up this Bible passage. What does it tell them about God?

What do the children feel when they sit on their mother's knee? What does this passage say about the writer's experience of the security and dependability of God?

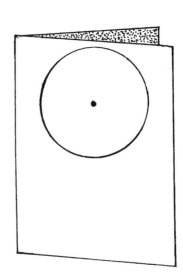

Psalm 131

O Lord, my heart is not lifted up,
my eyes are not raised too high;
I do not occupy myself with things too great
and too marvellous for me.
But I have calmed and quieted my soul,
like a child quieted at its mother's breast;
like a child that is quieted is my soul.
O Israel, hope in the Lord
from this time forth and for evermore.

(RSV)

Thank you card

Talk with the children about their mothers. What can they say thank you to her for on Mothering Sunday? Today most mothers manage to combine a number of different roles – carer, cook, nurse, story-teller, home-keeper, negotiator, judge, gardener, organizer, animal welfare officer, etc., and often work outside the home. They are often great jugglers who manage to do a number of different jobs at once. The children can make this simple card to say 'thank you' to their mothers who manage to keep so many 'balls' in the air at once. Younger children will need help in preparing the cards or to have the cards prepared for them to colour in.

You will need

two pieces of A4 card for each child

scissors

drawing and colouring materials

a 2p coin

compass

paper fasteners

METHOD

*   Fold a sheet of A4 paper in half.
*   Open the compass to 7 cm and draw a circle on the second piece of card measuring 14 cm in diameter. Cut this out.
*   Place the circle on the front of the card so that the top of the card is level with the top of the circle (fig. a). Where the compass-point has pierced the centre of the circle carefully pierce the front of the card behind it with the compass-point.
*   Place the card circle inside the card and with a paper fastener secure the circle to the pierced hole in the card. At the top centre of the card cut out a 3-cm box as shown (fig. b).
*   The centre circle can now act as a turning dial.
*   Turn the dial to reveal the blank card underneath the cut-out square and draw around a 2p to make a ball shape. Repeat this several times so that as the dial turns different balls appear.
*   Draw the mother figure and the juggling balls (drawing around a 2p coin) on the front of the card (fig. c).
*   Ask the children to consider all the different things that their mothers do. They can

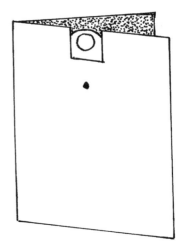

Fig. a

Fig. b

Fig. c

fill in each ball, including those on the turning dial, with a symbol or small picture of each of the different things.
- They should mark the inside of their cards with a greeting.

Decorated vases

Many congregations hand out posies of flowers on Mothering Sunday for children to give to their mothers. The week before Mothering Sunday the children can make these vases to put the flowers in.

METHOD
- Ask the children to design a decorated vase for their mothers.
- Those using glass paints will need careful supervision. Follow the instructions which come with the paints. When using these for the first time stick to a few simple outlines filled in with bold colours.
- The younger children can use the sticky collage materials to make a vase.
- Allow to dry.

You will need

clean, clear empty jam jars

for older children – glass paints, outliners and paintbrushes. The minimum suggested is three colours and one outliner.

for younger children – sticky collage materials

table coverings and aprons

kitchen roll

Oscar Romero

Martyr for liberation

Archbishop
Oscar Romero
Photo: *Cafod*

O scar Romero was appointed the Roman Catholic Archbishop of San Salvador in El Salvador, Central America, in 1977. Many people thought that the new Archbishop would keep the Church well away from controversial and political issues and not champion the needs of the poor as many priests had done. But three weeks after his appointment Oscar Romero had a life-changing experience. On 12 March 1977 his friend, Rutilio Grande, a Jesuit priest, was violently murdered. Father Grande had worked tirelessly with landless peasants and was often in trouble with the government authorities and security forces for his work and for speaking out against injustice. Although he was an educated man he had chosen to live with the poor and share their suffering because of his faith.

For the new Archbishop this priest's death was a shock and a challenge to his understanding of what was happening in his country. At the age of 59 Oscar Romero found a new way of being a Christian and understood his ministry as an Archbishop in a different way. He went against the views of some of his bishops and proclaimed three days of mourning for the murdered priest and held a funeral Mass in San Salvador's Cathedral. From this time the Archbishop became a 'voice of the voiceless' in El Salvador. He wrote letters urging the government, the military and people to talk to each other. He spoke out against the concentration of wealth amongst the privileged few and fought for the rights of the poor and oppressed. He condemned the false peace of the country which was kept in place by repressive policies and fear.

This prophetic witness of a once conservative bishop became a major threat to the government. The Roman Catholic radio station and weekly newspaper were attacked. The Jesuit university was bombed. But the Archbishop would not be stopped. He saw poverty as a sin, as an offence against God. His struggle for justice and lasting peace came from his religious understanding. He believed that people and institutions could change. He worked to realize the good news of the gospel for all the people of El Salvador. He made many enemies amongst the powerful and rich and even in the Church, but he continued to speak out. His courageous witness was to cost him his life. On 24 March 1980 Archbishop Romero was gunned down while he celebrated a Requiem Mass.

THEMES

The anniversary of Oscar Romero will often fall during Lent. These themes and activity ideas can be used to celebrate the life of Oscar Romero and to explore some of the traditional Lenten themes.

Change of heart – Lent is traditionally a time of penance, a time of turning away from sin and turning towards God. This repentance, or change of heart, was experienced by Oscar Romero at the death of his friend. He recognized that sin was not only something within each individual but within society itself. Christians needed to repent of their own sin but recognize that they also play their part in the sins of society.

Witness – Oscar Romero's life changed because of the life and witness of Rutilio Grande. Oscar Romero in turn, through his life and witness, changed other people's lives. His witness showed people that God did care for them, that the Church was concerned about poverty and injustice. Witnessing the faith means more than telling the gospel. For some like Oscar Romero it means shaking the establishment and shocking those in power.

Injustice – for Oscar Romero injustice was a sin, an offence against God. He saw poverty and injustice as a denial of God's will, a perversion of his creation.

TIMING

The salt dough crosses need at least two sessions to complete. The witness song can form part of a session. The good news–bad news frieze will take two sessions.

Activity ideas

Salt dough crosses – for older children

These salt dough crosses can be used to help illustrate the themes of repentance and a change of heart. This mixture is enough to make ten crosses.

METHOD

- Mix the flour and the salt in a large bowl.
- Add the oil and slowly add the water to make a stiff dough.
- Knead for ten minutes until you have a firm smooth dough. If it is a bit dry or cracks easily add more oil or water, but be careful not to add too much. The dough consistency is stiff.
- Divide the dough into ten balls and ask each child to continue to knead it until it is smooth.
- Place the ball of dough between two sheets of baking parchment. Over the paper carefully roll out the dough to a 0.5-cm thickness.
- Place the template on the dough and cut around it.
- Carefully push a paper clip into the dough at the top of the cross.
- Place the completed cross on the baking parchment and then on a baking sheet.
- Cook at 80°C for about five hours. Ovens vary so check the models after three hours.
- After three hours, using oven gloves carefully turn the models over on the sheet to dry out the underside.
- The models are cooked when it is not possible to pierce them with a pin.
- Remove the tray from the oven with oven gloves and cool.

To paint and varnish the models:

- The children can then paint their crosses with symbols and pictures on the front which remind them of Archbishop Oscar Romero. They could include his name, or the name of the country, a mitre, a gun.
- Once dry the back of the models can be painted/varnished in a plain colour.

You will need

plenty of adult supervision

aprons, oven gloves and table coverings

a large bowl and spoon

225 g plain flour

100 g salt

150 ml lukewarm water

2 tablespoons oil

baking parchment and paper clips

rolling pins and knives

copies of the template

baking sheets

paints ('Deco gloss' paints work well), paintbrushes

USING THE CROSSES

Discuss with the group how Oscar Romero followed Christ and had a change of heart that eventually led to his death. Sometimes the Christian faith can mean that difficult decisions have to be made.

Ask the group to use their cross in Lent as a focus for prayer. Their crosses made of bread dough can remind them that Oscar Romero fought so that everyone should have enough for their daily bread. Encourage the children to look at their crosses every night and think of one incident during the day when they did something wrong and did not show Jesus' love to others, and of an incident when they helped someone or did something for someone else. Remind them that Jesus will forgive their wrongdoing if they say they are sorry and change their ways.

A witness song – for mixed ages

The saints and the holy men and women of God are often people who shake the established way of doing things. St Francis shocked his father and his community by giving up his riches for a life of poverty for Christ. Rutilio Grande's death shocked Oscar Romero. He was so shaken by the incident that he began to consider his own life. His later martyrdom shocked the people of the world and caused many in the Church and government to reconsider their beliefs and actions. This dramatic form of witness is not what every Christian is called to do but throughout religious history there have been those 'movers and shakers' who have upset the established norm and enabled people to think again about their beliefs in a fresh way.

You will need

copies of the song

empty plastic bottles

dried peas

Thank you God

Thank you God for all your Saints

Thank you God for all you've done

Thank you God for Os - car Rom - er - o
Fran - cis of As - sisi, etc.

the shak - ers and the mov - ers for God Yes!

This simple song can be sung by the group and verses can be added to fit the third line. If there is time shakers can be made from empty plastic bottles containing dried peas. Encourage the group to dance around the room to the song, shaking their instruments as they go.

A good news/bad news frieze – for all ages

MAKING THE FRIEZE – WEEK 1

Archbishop Romero was a famous preacher. His Sunday sermons were broadcast nationally by the Church's own radio station. It is believed that 73 per cent of the rural population and 43 per cent of the urban population regularly tuned into the Mass at the Cathedral to hear the sermon. During these sermons the Archbishop recounted the *hechos de la semana* ('the events of the week') which was a recital of both the good and the bad news. In these sermons he denounced the evils of El Salvador and encouraged people to hear the good news of Christ and work to change the injustice around them.

The group can make their own 'good news/bad news' frieze to remind them that God is concerned for the whole of his creation.

> The world of food and work, of health and housing, the world of education – this is God's world . . . Poverty and desolation is a denial of God's will, a perverted creation in which God's glory is mocked and scorned.
>
> From a lecture given by Archbishop Romero, 2 February 1980

You will need

a Bible

a large sheet of stiff white paper or a roll of plain wallpaper

a sheet of white paper for each child

glue, scissors, colouring materials

METHOD

- Ask each child to draw a large outline of themselves on the sheet of paper.
- Ask them to write or draw on their picture something which has been good and bad about their week.
- Encourage them to draw their own facial features on their picture.

Older children – news gathering

Then divide the older children into two groups – the local group and the international group.

- Ask the groups to look through the newspapers or watch the TV news during the following week.
- Ask them to make a list of events and a selection of cuttings about local and international incidents which show unfairness or injustice in the world – the bad news.
- Ask them to make a similar selection of clippings which show the good news of the week.

MAKING THE FRIEZE – WEEK 2

Younger children

- Help the younger children to write in large letters at the top of the frieze 'Good news/bad news in God's world'.
- They can decorate the letters.
- Then they can glue the people figures made the previous week at the bottom of the frieze.

Older children

Discuss the cuttings and lists that the older children have brought in. What are the particular areas of injustice in their own local community? What have they identified as being unjust in the world? Are they able to do anything about it?

Talk about the quote from Oscar Romero above. What does Oscar Romero say about poverty? Explain to the group that Christians believe that they must work to make God's world a place which reflects his glory. Poverty, injustice and unfairness all work against God's will and creation. Discuss with them ways in which they are able to work for a fairer world in their own homes, in the local school or community and even in the wider world. Remind them of the different agencies which work to overcome injustice in the world.

COMPLETING THE FRIEZE

After the discussion the older children can glue their cuttings on to the frieze above the people templates and under the decorated letters.

Good Friday

A three-hour workshop

A Good Friday display of posters and lanterns by the children of St Stephen's Church, Worcester
Photo: *Robin Sharples*

Church children's groups often finish the passion story on Palm Sunday and go straight into Easter the following week. Because Good Friday falls in the school holidays, but not on a Sunday, it is often not observed by children. These workshop suggestions are designed so that the story of Good Friday is seen as part of a continuous narrative which leads to Easter. These ideas are designed to fill a three-hour workshop. They could take place from 12.00 until 3.00 whilst a three-hour devotion is taking place in church. The children could bring their own packed lunch. The material can be adapted for shorter sessions but ideally the activities should end with a short worship service.

THEMES

The Good Friday narrative has far more themes than can possibly be explored in a three-hour session. The ones which are explored here are:

The cross – these activities look at the symbol of the cross: what it signified in Jesus' time, different types of cross and what the cross may mean to children today.

Betrayal/denial – Jesus was betrayed by Judas, and denied by Peter and the crowd. These activities explore the idea of betrayal in drama and look at the consequences of it.

TIMING

The workshop is designed to fill three hours. The event needs to start with the welcome, followed by telling the story. Hot cross bun-making must come next to allow time for the buns to cook and cool before the children go home. The workshop needs to conclude with the worship. The other activities can be adapted and done in a different order. One suggestion is that the group is divided into two after a music session. While one group rehearses the drama another makes the lanterns and then they swap activities. Working with a large group to rehearse the drama should be avoided as the children may get bored waiting for their turn.

IN ADVANCE OF THE EVENT

- Send out invitations giving the place, timing and content of the event.
- These invitations should also include a consent form for the parents to sign as the event will last for three hours. See consent forms and sample invitation given in Appendices A and B (pages 103–5). Invite the parents and families of the children to the worship at the end of the event.
- Enlist the help of plenty of volunteers, arrange refreshments and collect the equipment needed.
- On the day set out the room and equipment, put the oven on and prepare the refreshments.

Welcome

Welcome the children to the workshop and introduce all the leaders who will be running the different activities. Explain that they will be looking at the story of Good Friday in many different ways. Outline the activities and explain that they will conclude with a short worship service. Give the group an idea about timings and the lunch break. Lunch could happen after the hot cross bun-making as the children will need to wash their hands after this activity.

Telling the story

Read the story of Judas' betrayal and the Good Friday story from St Matthew's Gospel chapters 26–27 from a children's Bible or show the group a video of the story. (Scripture Union produce a suitable video entitled *Good Friday – Easter Sunday,* price £14.99.) After the story explain that the activities they will be doing will remind them about the cross, Jesus' betrayal by Judas and denial by Peter and the crowd, and the first Easter.

You will need

video and video recorder if appropriate
chairs
drinks for the children
children's Bible

Making hot cross buns

In advance of the workshop prepare some hot cross bun dough from first principles or use a packet mix and add dried fruit. Make up a quantity of short-crust pastry. Allow each child enough dough to make two buns and a small amount of pastry.

Assemble the group and remind them why people make hot cross buns for Good Friday.

METHOD

- The children should first wash their hands.
- Ask the children to knead their dough balls and make two small rolls.
- They can then make two 'sausages' of pastry for each roll to make the cross shape.
- Using the glaze they can attach a cross to each bun and glaze the rest of their buns.
- Place the buns on a lined baking sheet, writing the child's name next to their bun on the lining, and cover. Leave to rise to twice their size in a warm place.
- Once risen show the children the buns.
- Place the buns in a hot oven until cooked – about twenty minutes.
- Cool and then wrap in kitchen paper for the children to take home.

Badge- and poster-making

Divide the group into two. One group can make badges and the other posters. Talk with the group about different cross shapes. Show them the selection you have brought in. Discuss these questions with them:

- What does each type of cross mean to them?
- Why are there different cross shapes?
- Which shape do they like and why?
- Why do Christians wear crosses or use crosses in church?

Explain how in Jesus' day crucifixion was used as a way of killing low-born criminals. Ask the children to make their own cross badge or poster.

Music session

Prepare two songs with instruments for the service. One song/hymn can be on the theme of Good Friday and one for Easter. This session can be divided into two smaller sessions, one immediately after lunch on the Good Friday theme and one later on the Easter theme.

Turn-around lanterns

Talk with the group about how the disciples must have felt when they realized that Jesus was going to be killed. Did they really believe that he would return to them? Then discuss the story of the first Easter morning. What do they think the women felt when they saw the empty tomb? This simple activity can remind the children about the stories.

METHOD

- Give each child a jam jar and ask them to place a small piece of Blu-Tack in the centre of the bottom of the jar.
- Carefully secure a night light on to the Blu-Tack.
- Give each child two small pieces of white paper.
- On one piece of paper they should draw a picture of the crucifixion.
- On the other piece they should draw a picture of the empty tomb.
- Glue these pictures either side of the lantern.

Explain that the lanterns will be used in the service. On the first Good Friday the world became dark, Jesus' followers had little hope. During the service the lanterns will be lit and turned around to show light shining out of the empty tomb. This will remind them that Jesus brought new life and hope into the world. He turned around people's understanding and brought light where there had been darkness.

You will need

jam jars
paper
glue and spreaders
Blu-Tack
night lights
taper and matches
scissors

Dramatic poem

There are four dramatic parts to the poem – Judas, Peter, the crowd and the soldiers. The leader can rehearse each of the parts separately with four different groups of children or rehearse two groups at a time while two groups are making lanterns. The props can be made in advance. Rehearse the chorus (in italic) with each group so that they get the rhythm. If there is a stage then 'Jesus' (either a mannequin or a volunteer person) can stand there while the children bring up the props. As each prop is mentioned one of the children can bring it up to the figure of Jesus and place it near or on him. Children can adapt and mime the poem or read it straight. The final part of the poem can be read by all the children during the service. It is helpful if this poem is mounted on an OHP so that the children can read it easily.

You will need

copies of the poem (or put on OHP)
mannequin or willing volunteer
bag of money
model of a crow
palms
scarlet cloak
crown made from twigs
kingly crown
white cloak

1. *This is the story of how Jesus died,*
He was put on the cross and crucified.
His friends betrayed him, they let him down,
The king they wanted wore a robber's crown.

Judas was the first friend to betray.
He was fed up with Jesus and tried to find a way
Of punishing the one they called Messiah
So the priests said to Judas – 'Yes you we'll hire'.

So Judas was paid 30 silver coins
For telling tales to the priests, the traitors he joins.
Judas told the enemies where Jesus would pray
And they went to arrest him without delay.

(Children take bag of coins to model.)

2. This is the story of how Jesus died,
He was put on the cross and crucified.
His friends betrayed him, they let him down,
The king they wanted wore a robber's crown.

Peter was the leader, they called him the rock,
And when he betrayed Jesus it came as a shock.
Jesus had warned him when the cock crowed three
He would remember his promise – 'Let you down? Not me!'

When the woman asked Peter if Jesus he did know,
Peter said 'Never seen him before', and turned to go.
The woman knew better and others knew him too
But Peter said 'He's not my friend, I haven't a clue.'

(Children take model of cock to the model.)

3. This is the story of how Jesus died,
He was put on the cross and crucified.
His friends betrayed him, they let him down,
The king they wanted wore a robber's crown.

When Jesus had arrived the crowd called him king,
They remembered David and his praises they did sing.
But the same crowd now shouted for him to die,
This was the king they would crucify.

Pilate appealed to them and asked if they were sure
But the crowd cried 'crucify him' all the more.
'Crucify him, crucify him,' they screamed out loud
'Hosanna', 'Crucify him', it was the same crowd.

(Children take palm and put it at the foot of the model.)

4. This is the story of how Jesus died,
He was put on the cross and crucified.
His friends betrayed him, they let him down,
The king they wanted wore a robber's crown.

The soldiers gave Jesus a thorny crown
They began to salute him, then bowed down
They beat him on the head and gave him a cloak
And with a stick they hit him and laughed at their joke.

They gave him wine mixed with myrrh to ease the pain
'If you are the King, they said, come down again.'
But Jesus died at the third hour
And it was three days later that God showed his power.

(Children take the crown of thorns and scarlet cloak and put them on Jesus.)

This is the story of how Jesus died,
He was put on the cross and crucified.
His friends betrayed him, they let him down,
The king they wanted wore a robber's crown.

(During the service the children can read the end of the poem and place the new props on Jesus.)

This story doesn't end there it continues to this day
Jesus was God's son, who came to show us the way.
We find it hard to follow, but he showed us what to do
The story of Easter is a story for you.

His crown of thorns became a kingly sight,
The day of darkness became a day of light.
This was the Christ, the expected king,
This is the Christ whose praises we sing.

(Replace crown of thorns with kingly and put on white robe.)

Jesus the king brought a new way of living,
Justice and peace and love and forgiving.
This was the Christ, the expected king.
This is the Christ whose praises we sing.

Service

The form and content of a concluding service need to be worked out between the leaders of the event. These are merely suggestions which worked with the trial group. Arrange the stage or central area with the posters made by the children. Arrange chairs for the children and adults to sit on.

- Assemble the group and ask them to process in, putting their lanterns on the central table/altar with the posters facing them.
- A leader then talks about what they have done during the day and why they have done it.
- Some of the children talk about their cross badges or posters.
- All sing a Good Friday hymn/song.
- The children act out the first part of the dramatic poem.
- An older child reads the Easter story.
- All the children sing an Easter hymn/song. While the children are singing a leader can light the lanterns and turn them round.
- An adult can then say a few short prayers which pick up the themes explored during the day.
- All the children act out the ending of the poem.

You will need

musical instruments and/or piano
song sheets or words on an OHP

Easter

'He is not here; for he has been raised, as he said' (Matthew 28.6 NRSV). The Easter message belongs to the central proclamation, the heart of the Christian faith. Unfortunately from the teaching point of view, the message is one which does not easily lend itself to being explained in simple terms. In raising Jesus from the dead God has acted in a new and unique way, so the teacher's method, beloved by Jesus himself, of saying 'X is like Y' and expressing one thing in terms of another is simply not appropriate. There is nothing like Easter. The contrast with the Passion and death of Jesus could hardly be more striking: we move from the drama of human suffering to the mystery of God who redeems.

THEMES

If the message of Easter is untranslatable and must be heard and encountered on its own terms, nevertheless the story of Christ's resurrection offers a rich source of themes. Those explored here are:

Surprise is too small a word for the amazement, wonder and downright disbelief of the followers of Jesus. Mark tells us they were too afraid even to pass the message on. God acts in a totally unexpected way, which only on reflection can be seen as entirely in keeping with a God who is love. **Continuity** is central to the gospel story, seen perhaps most graphically through Thomas's response and subsequent encounter with the risen Lord who bears the marks of crucifixion on his resurrection hands, feet and side (John 20.24ff.). At the same time there is **transformation** as the crucified body becomes the resurrection body.

TIMING

Each of these activities will take a session to prepare. The transformation picture for younger children will need some preparation in advance of the session.

Activity ideas
Easter crackers

METHOD

- Adults should help the children score the card across the diagonal using a ruler and knife.
- Fold the card to form a hinged triangle.

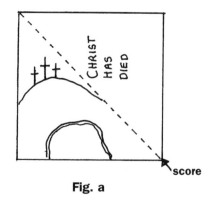

Fig. a

You will need for each child

one square of stiff card measuring 20 cm x 20 cm

one paper square the same size

sticky tape

drawing materials

ruler

a knife for scoring

scissors

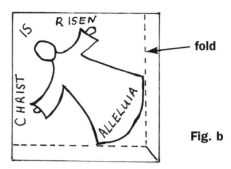

Fig. b

- On one of the outside sides of the hinged triangle ask the children to draw a picture of the hill of Calvary with three crosses in the background and a tomb in the foreground. On the other side of the triangle they should write 'Christ has died' (fig. a).
- On the paper square ask the children to draw a risen Christ as shown with the words 'Christ is Risen, Alleluia' (fig. b).
- Fold the paper in half to form the same size of triangle. Snip 1.5 cm into the end of the fold to create two 'flaps'.
- Fold the flaps parallel to the edge of the paper and using sticky tape place the paper over the card, fold to fold, and attach the flaps to the edge.
- Fold the hinge to enclose the paper in the card.
- Hold the card by the open corner, raise the cracker to head height and pull it very sharply down (fig. c). The paper will be forced out of the card case with a loud bang (fig. d).

The cracker aims to convey an idea of the surprise the apostles experienced when they realized that Christ had risen.

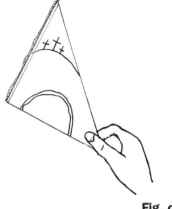

Fig. c

Fig. d

'Crucified and risen' transformation pictures – for younger children

METHOD

- An adult should cut out the photocopies of figures e and f (see pages 42 and 43). Cut out the shaded part of each drawing.
- Cut along the black lines at the top and bottom of figure f.
- Ask the children to slot figure e into slot 1 on figure f. Then thread figure e up through slot 2 as shown in figure g.
- The children can then move their models up and down to see that the crucified becomes the risen Jesus.
- Ask them to colour in their transformation scenes and show others how the crucified Lord and the risen Lord are one.

You will need for each child

photocopies of figs e and f overleaf

drawing materials

scissors

He is crucified

He is risen

Fig. e

Jesus is Lord

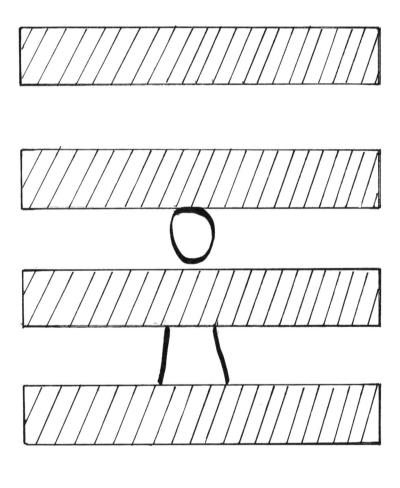

Fig. f

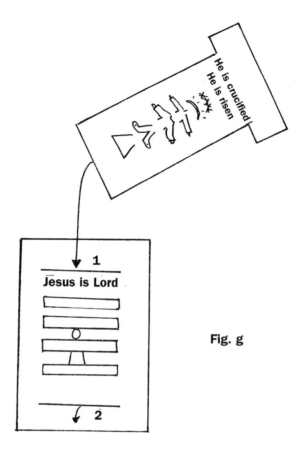

Fig. g

For older children

A more intricate artefact of continuity/newness/transformation is this Easter folder. It is tricky to make and the children will need to measure and fold carefully.

METHOD

- On each card square make two folds a quarter (2.5 cm) of the way along the length by folding two sides so that they meet in the middle (fig. h).
- Cut the cards across the middle of the squares as shown. Unfold so that there is a total of four identical rectangles (fig. i).
- Put the rectangles together again to form the two squares. Now place one square on top of the other with their cuts at right angles.
- With a stapler, secure each of the four corners together (fig. j).
- The resultant device can be folded in a variety of configurations.
- Fold it first into a cross shape with the split vertical. On this shape draw the figure of Jesus with the legend 'Jesus is crucified' (fig. k).
- Open the cross to find a square with the split horizontal and draw Calvary, with the three crosses on the hill and the tomb in the foreground and the legend 'Jesus is buried in the tomb' (fig. l).
- Open the picture to find the vertical split and draw the empty tomb with the disciples and the legend 'His friends look for his dead body but . . .' (fig. m).
- Open the picture again and on the central panel draw the risen Christ with the legend 'Christ is Risen. Alleluia' (fig. n).
- The children now have a pocket-sized version of the Easter transformation story.

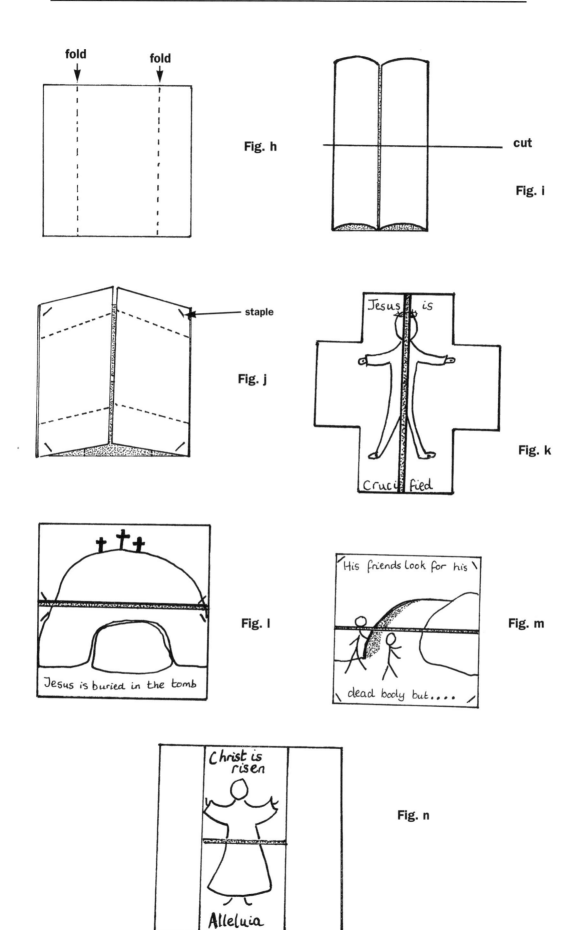

fold   fold

Fig. h

cut

Fig. i

staple

Fig. j

Jesus is

Crucified

Fig. k

Jesus is buried in the tomb

Fig. l

His friends look for his

dead body but....

Fig. m

Christ is risen

Alleluia

Fig. n

Pentecost

The Church seems to specialize in using exotic and mysterious-sounding names that turn out to have very simple explanations. One such word is 'Pentecost', which simply means 'the fiftieth day'. In the Jewish tradition, seven weeks after the Passover saw the celebration of the 'Feast of Weeks', originally a harvest festival but by the time of Christ principally a commemoration of the giving of the Law to Moses. The Acts of the Apostles tells us that it was on this day that the Holy Spirit came upon the twelve disciples with wind and fire and transformed them from a small group of followers of Jesus into a missionary movement which went out into all the known world. The catalogue of countries listed in Acts (Acts 2.9ff.), which tests the nerve and twists the tongue of anyone who has to read the passage out loud, was a kind of A–Z of the known world.

The Old English name for Pentecost is rather more transparent. Whit Sunday simply meant 'White Sunday' because many baptisms were performed – appropriately linking the gift of the Spirit to the whole Church with the gift of the Spirit to the individual – and candidates traditionally wore white as a sign of purity. The liturgical colour for altar frontals and vestments is red, symbolic of the fire that appeared on the heads of the twelve.

The modern Pentecost is still the fiftieth day after Easter, but the official Bank Holiday now falls on the last Monday in May which does not always coincide with Whit Monday. In the North of England, especially round Manchester, the festival is still celebrated with processions of Christian witness, the Whit Walks.

THEMES

Pentecost is the celebration of the gift of the Holy Spirit to the Church and indeed it is frequently called the 'birthday of the Church'. This title is somewhat misleading because other events in the gospels could be regarded as the moment when the Church was born, e.g. the gift by Jesus of the Holy Spirit and the power to forgive or retain sins (John 20.22). Power and energy are symbolized by the wind and fire familiar in Old Testament imagery. The gift of 'speaking in tongues' as described in Acts was not the unintelligible ecstatic utterance which caused St Paul so many problems: it was rather the ability to communicate the good news of Jesus Christ to the whole world. God speaks to us human beings, in all our diversity, in ways which we can understand – one gospel, many forms of expression. So we can draw on the theme of **language** and on the theme of **diversity in unity.** Through making bishops' mitres children can explore the idea of the **power of the spirit.**

TIMING

Each of the craft activities can take one session.

Activity ideas

Starting the session

Sing the following, line by line, with the children repeating each line in turn. It might take a couple of goes, but young children latch on to sounds very quickly without even thinking of them as 'foreign' languages. Sing it to the tune of 'London's Burning'.

Good morning, good morning
Guten Morgen, Guten Morgen,
Bonjour, Bonjour,
Buenos Dias, Buenos Dias.

Explain that the words mean the same in English, German, French and Spanish: different sounds, but the same idea of greeting. Now sing it as a round. Everyone knows what the words mean, and the variety of languages makes them sound more beautiful and interesting than if they were only sung in English. The song provides a good introduction to the reading of Acts 2.1-11. Explain that verses 9-11 are meant to tell us that every country in the world was represented. Perhaps the apostles, preaching sounded a bit like the round the children have just sung: different languages, but everyone understood.

The Pente-cross collage – for younger children

Talk to the children about different countries they have visited or seen on television, or where they have relatives. Ask them about different things they noticed in these countries – language, food, customs, scenery – to get across the idea of the variety of human life. If you have the chance to prepare, ask them a week in advance to bring in photographs or postcards and other pictures. If not, the best source of material is your local travel agent.

You will need

A large piece of card
travel brochures
scissors
drawing materials
glue and spreaders
ruler
piece of card
Blu-Tack

METHOD

- Draw a large cross on the card.
- Ask the children to cut and paste, or Blu-Tack, their pictures on to the cross.
- Ask them to write on the names of the countries they have selected near the pictures.
- Mount the cross so that it is visible for everyone to see.

Explain to the group how the first apostles took the story of Jesus to the whole world. Since those days other Christians have worked to make sure that the Church can be found in every country. The apostles' message was that Jesus was killed on a cross and God gave him new life: so they believed, as Christians today believe, that 'Jesus is Lord'. Ask the group to write this above, under or around their Pente-cross. Read the second collect for Pentecost Sunday (ASB, page 635) changing the word 'men' to 'people'. You could sing at this point 'Alleluia, Alleluia, give thanks to the risen Lord'.

A variation on the theme: the Whit House

The teaching of this activity is the same as the Pente-cross.

METHOD

- Place the banana boxes side by side on their sides to form a single box and use strong tape to form a 'hinge'.
- Cover the outsides of the box with white paper and paint windows on the side and a door at the opposite end to the hinge so that the boxes look like an opened-up church.
- The children can add their pictures or cut-outs from brochures and glue them inside the 'church'.
- Make two strips of paper to stick above the 'door' on either side. On one strip write 'Jesus is Lord' and on the other 'All Welcome'.
- Display the international church hinged open in your own church.

You will need
two banana boxes
strong wide tape
white paper
travel brochures
scissors
glue and spreaders
drawing materials

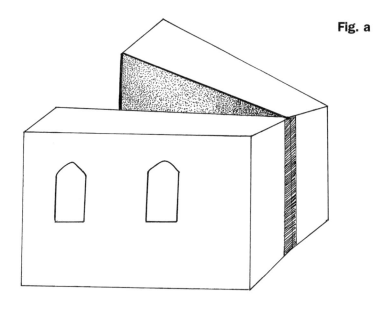

Fig. a

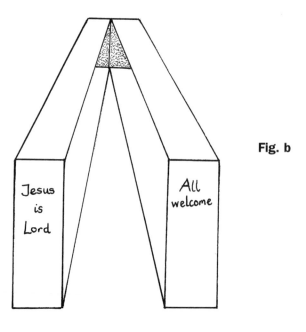

Fig. b

Jesus
is
Lord

All
welcome

Heads aflame!
The bishop's mitre – for older children

Read Acts 2. Explain to the group that the Church was not started because someone thought it would be a good idea: it was started because God gave the people who had followed Jesus power and energy to go out and tell others about him. The Holy Spirit is often called God's 'power' or God's 'energy'. The sign that they had been given this power was that they appeared to have flames of fire resting on their heads as if they were 'on fire' with the Spirit.

In today's Church it is often the bishops who lead the preaching of the gospel, so they are the successors of those first Church leaders. One of the reasons for having bishops is to show the link with the apostles at Pentecost. This continuity is called the 'apostolic succession'. As a sign of the work of the Holy Spirit, and also to show that today's bishops lead the modern Church as the apostles led the first Church, bishops wear a special kind of hat called a mitre. It is shaped like a flame.

You will need
tape measure
large sheets of card
scissors
staples and stapler
drawing materials
sticky tape

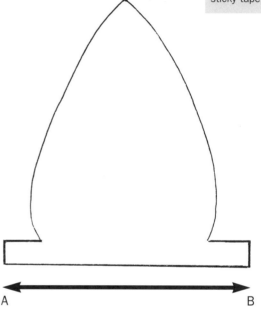

Discuss with the group the reading. What were the signs of the Spirit? – Wind, fire, languages. What happened to the apostles? – They went out preaching 'Jesus is Lord' to all the known world. You may also want to look at other 'signs' of the Holy Spirit in scripture – the dove, for instance. Using these ideas get the children to decorate mitres.

METHOD

- Ask the children to measure around their heads and divide that measurement in half.
- The distance between point A and point B needs to be half the circumference measurement of the child's head plus 6 cm.
- Cut two mitre outlines for each child.
- Overlap the tabs of the mitre by 3 cm on each side and secure with staples. Use sticky tape to cover the staple ends.
- Ask the children to colour in their mitres using the symbols of the Holy Spirit or colours of fire.

Bede

Father of English History

The Venerable Bede. *From Andre Thevet, Les Vrais Portraits et Vies des Hommes Illustres, 1584* Photo: *The Mary Evans Picture Library*

The Father of English History' and chronicler of events of great importance, Bede himself lived a life that is remarkable for its uneventfulness. A monk by vocation and, so far as we can tell, also by disposition, he spent his days devoted to the disciplines of prayer and study. Perhaps it was the very still-ness and calm of his own life which made him such an acute observer and accurate reporter of the world around him and of the stories he gathered of the history of the Church.

Bede was born in Northumberland in AD 673 and had his first association with monastic life as a child aged seven, being educated at the monasteries of Wearmouth and Jarrow. He became a monk at Jarrow in AD 682, but was not ordained until some twenty years later. Monks were not usually ordained priests in those days and his title 'Venerable', commonly applied to priests, distinguished him from the other brothers.

His *Church History* traces the Christian story in England. Completed in AD 731 it is still the single most important source for the period, and despite its limitations, its methodology – quoting sources and analyzing the evidence – justifies Bede's description, not merely as the first Church historian of England, but as the Father of English History. He was the first historian to designate the years since the birth of Jesus as 'AD' Anno Domini, Year of our Lord. Yet for all that, and for all his copious writings on a wide range of subjects, this devoted holy man regarded as his most important work his commentaries on the Bible, 25 in all. In his last days he was engaged in translating St John's Gospel, just managing to complete it before his death. The monk Cuthbert records that he died singing a 'Gloria'.

THEMES

Both monk and historian have a special concern for time: the latter follows events and peoples as time progresses; the former lives by a rule in which time is strictly ordered to allow for prayer, study and work. **Time** is therefore a central theme in discussing Bede, and the activities suggested are designed to explore both approaches.

The cards idea draws on the use we make of cards to mark both the passage of time (birthdays, wedding anniversaries) and the occasions of special significance in our lives (birth, baptism, confirmation, moving house and passing exams). The purpose of these cards is to show that we each have our own history and that our history is with God.

'A cycle of time' shows older children how the Church keeps all time as God's time. The liturgical calendar marks the most important events in the life of Jesus Christ and therefore in the history of salvation.

Bede took enormous trouble to record events, and his work has been preserved. He also wrote extensively in Old English, but all this work has been lost. We need historians to record and and also to preserve knowledge about the past. Without proper care so much information, so many documents can simply disappear. The theme of the **need for care**, and of the fragility of our records, is illustrated by the **history of the community** activity.

TIMING

Each activity will take one session. To make the parchment an oven will have to be put on before the session begins.

Activity ideas
Time:
A Christian history card – for younger children

In some groups all the children will have been baptized. In this case the leader can record the dates of their baptisms and the children can make cards for each other which say '. . . years with Jesus'.

In other groups there will be some children who have been baptized and others who have not and are not regular attenders. The leader will need to be sensitive to this situation and this group could make event cards inscribed 'Happy Church Day' in which the children celebrate their participation in church that day.

God's time:
A cycle of time – for all ages

METHOD

* Give each child the two card circles and ask them to secure the centre point through each of them with a paper fastener so that they can spin the smaller circle.

You will need

a piece of card folded in half for each child

drawing and colouring materials

You will need for each child

two card circles – one 20cm in diameter, the other 30cm

a paper fastener

colouring and drawing materials

scissors

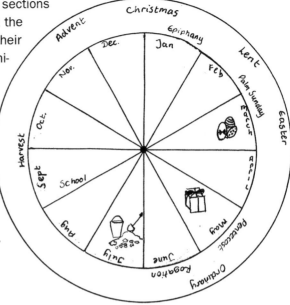

- Ask them to mark the smaller circle with sections for each of the months and then to mark the significant dates within those months – their birthday, the birthdays of friends and families, holiday dates etc.
- On the larger circle they should mark the seasons of the Christian year (see page 17 of *The Christian Year: Calendar, Lectionary and Collects*).
- If they want to they can colour these seasons with the appropriate liturgical colours (see page 14 of the same book).
- Remind them that all time is God's time.

A history of the local community – for older children

This activity can form part of a larger project on the history of a local community. Just as Bede believed that it was important to write down the history of the English Church before it was forgotten, so the children can hear about 'the old days' from older members of the community or from local history books and so understand something about their own history as a community.

In advance of the session find out about the history of your local church or community or ask the children to. You might decide to find out about a series of buildings or well-known local people from the past. Encourage the children to find out as much as possible about one person in their local history. The children can then write an imaginary diary of the person they have chosen on a piece of 'parchment'.

You will need for the 'parchment'
sheets of thick white paper or watercolour paper
a pot of strained strong tea
an oven
baking trays
pens and colouring materials

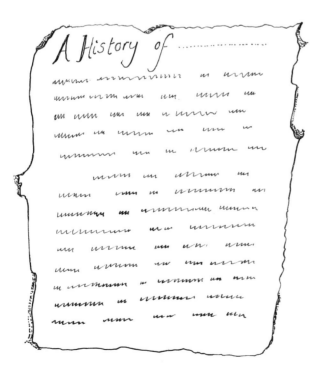

METHOD

- Fill a baking tray with tea. Take a piece of paper, watercolour paper works best, and tear the edges so that they are ragged. Soak in the tea for a couple of minutes.
- Shake the excess tea off the paper and place on a dry baking tray.
- 'Cook' or dry out the paper in a moderately hot oven and get an adult to carefully remove the paper when it has gone brown.
- Once the paper has cooled down the children can write their own historical documents.

Bernard Mizeki

African martyr

Bernard Mizeki
Photo: *Estudio Corte Real, Maputo*

Little is known about the early life of Bernard Mizeki. His family came from a small village in the Bay of Inhambane in modern Mozambique. He was born in the 1860s and given the name Mamiyeri Mizeki Gwamba. When he was young his father died so he went to live with his uncle. At first he worked in the local trading store. When he was about twelve years old he joined his cousin and some other young boys and ran away from the village. The boys went by ship to Cape Town where they found work. Soon they came under the influence of the Society of St John the Evangelist – 'the Cowley Fathers'. Mizeki joined his friends in a night school run by Fräulein von Blomberg for the mission. It is from Miss von Blomberg's writings that we learn about Mizeki's early life. His teacher tells how he was fascinated by the Scripture class. She remembers telling the class how God knew each of them and loved them. Bernard exclaimed: 'This is something I did not know! I ought to have done something for God, working for Him and serving Him, if He cares for me so much. Do tell Him that I am very sorry that I haven't done anything for Him yet, but I didn't know about Him at all.'

Mizeki was baptized on 7 March 1886. In 1891 Bishop Knight Bruce went to Cape Town to find volunteers for his pioneer missionary work in Mashonaland (in modern Zimbabwe). When Bernard offered himself for service his friends and teachers asked whether he were not afraid to go so far from his home: 'Why should I be afraid? It is my will to serve God, because He first did so much for me. Only now can I really start work, and Mashonaland is no further from heaven than Cape Town!'

Bernard Mizeki shrine Photo: *Jon Williams*

The missionaries sailed to Beira in modern Mozambique from where they travelled by steamer, wagon and on foot for hundreds of miles. The Bishop and Bernard went to see Chief Mangwende, ruler of the WaNhowe tribe and explained the object of their mission to him. The chief welcomed Bernard and a place was found for him to live. Records about Bernard's mission are plentiful. His gift for languages proved invaluable as he quickly mastered the language of the local Shona people and became known as the best interpreter. Soon he began his translation work. His musical gifts were also popular: he was later remembered as the one who introduced tonic sol-fa to the village. At first the people were suspicious of him but Bernard won their confidence. Mangwende declared that every Sunday was a holiday and no work should be done. Bernard became known as an excellent teacher and a man of great faith and austerity. Bernard married Mutwa, a granddaughter of Mangwende. They were to be married for only three months.

Matabele War

In 1893 the Matabele rose up against the white settlers. When the war ended Matabeleland, Mashonaland and Manicaland were united and the whole area named Rhodesia. But the Matabele people remembered their former power, and the peace did not last long. The Matabele, traditionally the enemies of the Mashona, sent their messengers to stir up the Mashona against the settlers. In March 1896 the Matabele revolted and killed white people throughout their area.

Mangwende's people were divided. Mangwende's brother, Gatzi, and his son, Mchemwa, held talks with the Matabele spies in the area. Mchemwa hated the white man, the mission, Bernard and his father. He collected guns and prepared for war. The n'anga (witchdoctor/healer) also used his power to stir up the people against Bernard. Baba Foster, the priest at Mutare, sent a messenger to all the catechists and teachers in the area telling them to go to Penhalonga for safety. Bernard refused to go. 'Mangwende's people are suffering. The Bishop put me here and told me to remain. Until the Bishop returns, here I must stay. I cannot leave my people now in a time of such darkness.'

The last days

One night there was a loud knocking on Bernard's hut door. Bernard eventually allowed his visitors in after they had tricked him. Zuite, Mangwende's son, and another man entered the hut and knocked Bernard over. Mutwa's other uncle Bodjgo then stabbed him with a spear and ran off. Mutwa thought Bernard was dead and she went to find her friend. The two women found Bernard on the hillside washing his wound. He was very weak and he pleaded with the women to hide themselves. Bernard spoke to Mutwa: 'Your uncles have attacked me and I am dying. I wish you to be baptized, and the child in your womb. The work of the priests and teachers is not ended. When I am dead more priests will come and one day all your people will be Christian.' The two women, seeing how weak he was, went to prepare him some food. When they returned a bright light almost blinded them. The hillside where Bernard had been left was lit up and there was a noise 'like many wings of great birds'. In the centre of the light where Bernard lay, there was a strange red glow. The women were frightened and hid themselves. When the light disappeared they could not find Bernard.

In the confusion of war, news of Bernard's death did not immediately reach the Church authorities. But then the story of Bernard Mizeki spread. Today on the Saturday nearest the date of Bernard's death on 18 June thousands of Christians gather every year near Marondera in Zimbabwe to remember this great apostle of the Christian faith.

THEMES

The story of the **courage** and **persistence** of Bernard Mizeki throughout his life has great potential for dramatic re-enactment. The other themes explored here are **doing something for God**, and his **love of music**.

TIMING

The drama can take ten minutes or more than one session depending upon how it is done. The music activity can form part of one session. The cloth-printing will take a whole session.

Activity ideas

Drama – for all ages

Discuss Bernard Mizeki's life with the group by asking them these questions to get them thinking about how to do a short play.

- How would they have felt leaving their family at the age of twelve to go on a boat to a strange country?
- What do they imagine happened when Bernard and his friends arrived in Cape Town?
- What do they think about Bernard's comment about doing something for God?
- What would Chief Mangwende have said to the Bishop and Bernard?
- Do they think that many people would have stayed behind to look after their people when it was so dangerous?
- What do they think about the end of the story when Bernard is killed?

Afterwards the children can rehearse a series of sketches about Bernard Mizeki's life. They might choose to write them down and rehearse them for a performance or simply act them out to each other.

Singing for God – for all ages

Bernard Mizeki was remembered by many people in Zimbabwe for his gift of languages and for teaching people the sol-fa. This activity combines these two themes. Bernard Mizeki knew many languages. He will have spoken the language of his people in Mozambique, English with the people at the Cowley Mission and the Shona language. He not only learnt the language of his adopted people but he learnt about their culture and their way of life in order that he could explain the Christian story in a way they would understand. Bernard also used music to pass on his message. This simple song – 'Thuma mina' – is a South African song and can be learnt by the children and sung.

Doing something for God: Cloth printing – for older children

You will need

an old cotton sheet

fabric paints

pencils

an iron and ironing board

table coverings

aprons

pictures of elephants, Bible, cross, outline of Africa, music notes

When Bernard Mizeki first heard the Christian story he was determined to 'do something for God'. Doing something for God need not necessitate becoming a brave and courageous missionary like Bernard Mizeki. For many people doing something for God can be a simple act – singing in the choir, helping a member of the community, decorating the church or visiting the sick. Christians try and spend their whole life 'doing something for God' although it is far from easy. This cloth-printing activity can be something the older group 'do for God'.

Thuma mina

Traditional South African

2 *Thuma mina Somandla*   2 Send me Jesus . . .

3 *Ronia nna Modimo*   3 Lead me Jesus . . .

4 Fill me Jesus . . .

Reproduced by permission of Walton Music Corporation.

METHOD

- Explain to the group that they are going to make an altar cloth or a display cloth for Bernard Mizeki's day. This cloth could be used in a service or simply as a reminder of someone who 'did something for God'.
- Ask the children to think about the things which they associate with Africa and then the things which they associate with Bernard Mizeki's life. In Zimbabwe every year there is a celebration for Bernard Mizeki's day. Men often wear specially printed T-shirts and women specially printed African cloths or kitenges with a picture of Bernard Mizeki on. Drawing a face in fabric paints can be tricky but the children can make their own cloth by outlining shapes and symbols in pencil on the cloth and filling them in with paint. Read the instructions on the fabric paints before starting to paint.
- Once completed the dried cloth can be ironed and displayed.

St Alban

Britain's first martyr

St Alban and Priest, *from Matthew Paris,* The Life of St Alban Photo: *The Board of Trinity College, Dublin*

According to Bede, Alban was a citizen of the Roman city of Verulamium (which lay outside the present city of St Albans) probably between AD 200 and AD 254. One day he gave shelter to a Christian priest who was escaping from people who wanted to kill him. Alban did not know about Christianity but was so impressed by the way the priest devoted himself day and night to continual prayer that he became a Christian. The rulers sent soldiers to find the priest but he and Alban changed clothes so the priest could escape. The soldiers, thinking that Alban was the priest, arrested him and took him to the judge. The judge was angry when he realized that he had got the wrong man and threatened Alban. When he asked Alban his name, Alban replied: 'My parents named me Alban, and I worship and adore the living, the true God, who created all things.' The judge ordered Alban to offer sacrifices to the Roman gods. Alban refused. The judge then ordered that Alban be flogged so that he would change his mind. Alban again remained true to his convictions and did not change his mind. The judge then ordered that Alban be beheaded but again he was thwarted. When the executioner heard Alban's story he too became a Christian and the judge became even more annoyed and had to find another executioner. Bede records that a number of miracles took place as Alban went to be beheaded. A fast-flowing river dried up so that people could cross it and follow Alban; as Alban asked God for water on top of the hill where he was to be martyred, a spring gushed up at his feet. When Alban was finally beheaded the eyes of the executioner dropped out. The judge was so alarmed by these miracles that he ordered an end to the persecution and began to respect the deaths of the martyrs. News about Alban's courage and bravery spread and St Albans became an important place for pilgrimage. The Roman bricks from the ruins of Verulamium were later used in the building of the great Norman Cathedral of St Albans.

THEMES

The rich and vivid story of St Alban as recounted by Bede provides plenty of themes for the children's leader.

God's power reigns supreme – the courage and humility of Alban is placed in sharp contrast to the power and arrogance of the judge. Yet the judge's power is constantly thwarted, almost comically so. God is shown continually to upset the judge's plans. First the judge gets the wrong man, who refuses to be frightened by his threats and who converts his executioner. Finally the judge gives in and respects the martyrs. The worldly power of the judge is no match for the power of God. This theme can be brought out in a dramatic presentation of the story.

Witness – St Alban is believed to be the first British martyr. The witness of the priest led to Alban's own conversion. Alban's witness and life then helped to convert his executioner and so begins a chain of witnesses who keep the story of Jesus alive. Although powerful rulers may kill individual Christians their story lives on.

Christians in Roman Britain – children often study the Romans as part of the history syllabus at school. The story of St Alban can provide a starting point for work on Christianity in Roman Britain.

TIMING

The drama and the Roman Britain activities will take a session. The picture chain and action song together will take a session.

Activity ideas

A St Alban's drama – for all ages

The story of St Alban lends itself to a dramatic presentation. Encourage the children to improvize the script and to show how God's power reigns supreme. You will need at least six characters: Alban, the priest, the judge, two executioners and a crowd.

Picture chain – for younger children

METHOD

Fig. a

- Fold a long strip of paper into five with concertina folds.
- Copy the outline of the person in figure a on to the front of the concertina. Make sure that the hands touch the fold of the paper.
- Cut out the figures.
- When unfolded there should be five figures holding hands.
- On the first figure ask the children to draw a picture of the priest that Alban sheltered. On the second they can draw Alban. On the third picture draw the executioner. On the fourth can be a picture of someone who watched the execution of Alban. On the final figure the children can draw a self-portrait.

You will need

long strips of white paper

scissors

colouring materials

Once completed the handing-on-the-faith picture chain can be used to show how the Christian faith is passed on from person to person. Although they have never met St Alban the children are also part of the same faith story which is passed on through generations.

Action song

Use the music for 'Here we go gathering nuts in May' for this action song idea. Run through the music and verses a couple of times with the group and then they can do the actions.

> Here is a story of long ago, long ago, long ago,
> Of a priest who told the story of Christ
> to a Roman soldier called Alban.

Here is a story of long ago, long ago, long ago,
Of Alban who told the story of Christ to his
Roman executioner.

Here is a story of long ago, long ago, long ago,
Of the executioner who told the story of Christ
to his family in St Albans.

Here is a story of long ago, long ago, long ago,
Of the family who told the story of Christ
to a builder in St Albans.

Here is a story of long ago, long ago, long ago,
Of the builder who told the story of Christ
through the Cathedral in St Albans.

The children can be encouraged to add their own verses to the song showing how the story of Christ was passed on through the generations.

ACTIONS

- Line the group up with a gap between each child.
- The child at the front of the line then has to weave in between the children linking hands with each of the children in the line.
- Once the verse for the priest is completed the song begins again and the next child in the line repeats the actions as St Alban and so on.

Discussion material – for older children

Little is known about the daily life of Christians who lived in Roman Britain. Clues about them survive from ecclesiastical writings and archaeological finds which date back to late Roman Britain. These finds include spoons, bowls, tombstones and lead tanks marked with Christian symbols, the Chi-Rho, the Alpha and Omega and the first words of the 'Our Father'.

The most dramatic archaeological find of the twentieth century was the discovery of the Mildenhall Treasure in the 1940s. This was a treasure trove of buried silver dating to the 360s. Most of the objects have no Christian significance but the treasure includes three spoons marked with the Greek Letters Chi (X) and Rho (P). Chi and Rho are the two Greek letters that begin the Greek word 'Christ'. Finds at Water Newton in Huntingdonshire in 1975 included a collection of Christian silver. These, like the triangular silver and gilt plaque illustrated, included the Chi-Rho symbol again. The plaque also shows the Alpha (A) and Omega (Ω), the first and last letters of the Greek alphabet, a reminder of the text from Revelation: 'I am Alpha and Omega, the beginning and the end' (Revelation 21.6). The Alpha and Omega often appear with the Chi-Rho on Roman Christian objects. Sometimes the lower case Omega (ω) appears with the upper case Alpha.

The earliest Christians often used symbols to show that something was for Christian use. Symbols are signs which have a special meaning. Discuss with the group what Christian symbols they are familiar with today. Show them the signs below and ask what they signify.

Triangular silver and gilt plaque from the earliest-known British hoard of Christian plate, from Water Newton, Cambridgeshire Photo: *1992, the Trustees of the British Museum.*

The **cross** is associated with the death of Jesus and was not used widely in Christian Roman art because it was associated with the death of a low-born criminal.

The **fish** was chosen by early Christians to represent Christ and was also sometimes used of the newly baptized and of the eucharist. The Greek word for fish – *ichthus* – is formed from the first letters of  the acrostic in Greek *Iesous Christos Theou Uios Soter* – Jesus Christ, Son of God, Saviour. A simple form of the *ichthus* was found incised on a block of stone at the Roman villa in Rockbourne, Hampshire.

The **Church of England logo** was designed in 1996 and combines the letters c and e with a cross.

The **Compassrose** is the logo of the Anglican Church worldwide. At the centre of the emblem is the red cross of St George on a silver shield. This serves as a reminder of the English origins of the Anglican Communion. Encircling the cross is a band with the Greek inscription translating as 'The truth shall make you free'. From this band radiate all the points of the compass, symbolizing the worldwide Anglican Church today.

Talk with the children about all these symbols. Ask them if they have a special way of signing their own name or a personal logo or symbol which says something about them. They can incorporate these symbols in a specially designed pencil holder.

A pencil holder

METHOD

- Cut out a piece of paper to fit around the jam jar.
- Ask the children to create a design on the paper using the Christian symbol they have chosen and their own initials or logo.
- Glue this paper around the jam jar.
- Use a strip of sticky-backed plastic to protect the drawing.

You will need
clean, empty jam jars
paper
drawing materials
scissors
glue and spreaders
sticky-backed plastic

St Benedict

A rule of life

St Benedict *by Hans Memling. Uffizi Gallery, Florence*
Photo: *AKG London*

It seems entirely in keeping with Benedict's temperament and wish that we know very little about his life, and yet that untold people since have been encouraged, inspired and even formed in the Christian faith by his lasting influence. Born around AD 480 in Nursia, Italy, and educated in Rome, he was appalled by the immoral way of life he found there. He became a hermit, living in utter solitude. But his piety became famous, and he attracted many disciples whom he organized into twelve monasteries of around twelve monks each. This was the beginning of monasticism in the Western Church, and Benedict is rightly celebrated as the founder of Western monasticism.

The precise reasons for his move to Monte Cassino are not clear: it seems a jealous priest was spreading rumours. Around AD 525 he took a band of monks to the place now associated with his name. It was here that he produced his famous 'Rule'. Steeped in Scripture, with a quotation or reference in nearly every sentence, the Rule is a guide to spiritual growth for the individual monk and a charter for the common life of the monastery. Though his own asceticism was severe, the Rule is marked by moderation and humanity. It aims for a balanced life consisting of prayer, study and manual work to occupy spirit, mind and body. The fact that it has endured for nearly 1500 years and is still in use today, both by Benedictine religious and by others seeking spiritual guidance, is ample testimony to Benedict's wisdom, insight and understanding. Benedict died around AD 550, but his tradition lives on.

THEMES

'So, brothers, if we wish to reach the highest peace of humility...then the ladder which appeared to Jacob in his dream...must be set up, so that we may mount by our own actions' (Chapter 7 of the Rule). 'Humility' lists the steps on the ladder 'that we go down through pride and up through humility', so humility is essential at each stage in prayer. The 'prayer ladder' is one means of exploring the theme of **prayer**, so central to Benedict; so too are the 'hand prayers'.

The Rule covers both personal piety and the practical organization of the community, even going into details about how much wine is to be allowed (half a pint per person per day) and about kitchen duties. Particular emphasis is placed upon hospitality, to such an extent that Chapter 56 requires the Abbot always to take his meals with guests or pilgrims, and if none are around he is to invite monks to stand in for them. Therefore the theme of **welcome and hospitality** is explored here.

TIMING

The prayer activities and welcome poster will both take part of one session.

Activity ideas
Prayer:
Ladder prayers – for older children

Remind the group about Benedict's teaching on prayer and the idea of ascending a ladder. Explain that there are different types of prayer, such as confession, supplication, thanksgiving and adoration. Explain that when Christians pray to God they often start by saying what they are sorry for (confession), then ask God for help (supplication); they often also give thanks to God for what they have received (thanksgiving) and finally they may make a prayer of adoration, of awe and wonder, a prayer without any self-interest. One way to visualize these different types of prayer is by making a ladder. Each rung can be a different type of prayer, and on each step Benedict reminds people that humility is central.

Ask the children to draw their own prayer ladder cards to remind them of this idea. On each rung of the ladder they can write 'humility' and between each rung they can write one of the different types of prayer.

Hand prayers – for younger children

METHOD

- Ask the children to draw around their left hand.
- They should then cut this shape out and trace around it on three pieces of paper. They should cut out these shapes so that they have four hands.
- Put the four hands together and with adult help staple down the straight left hand side of the hand as shown.
- In this book of hands the children can write their own four types of prayer. A prayer which says they are sorry for something, a prayer which asks for God's help, a prayer of thanksgiving and a prayer of adoration.

You will need

sheets of paper
drawing materials
scissors
stapler

Welcome posters – for all ages

To remind the group about the importance of **welcome and hospitality** in Benedict's teaching the children can make their own welcome poster. This can be displayed in the entrance to the church or class and list the time and place of the group's meeting or special event.

You will need

large sheet of card
collage materials or different coloured papers
glue
drawing materials
scissors

METHOD

- Ask the children to outline the letters which spell 'welcome'.
- They can then fill these in with different collage materials and glue them to the card.
- If appropriate they can add the time and place of their meeting or design leaflets which welcome other children to join their group.
- The welcome poster can then be displayed in a prominent place in church or the school.

William Wilberforce

Campaigner for the abolition of slavery

William Wilberforce Photo: *The Church Missionary Society*

Villiam Wilberforce was one of the great evangelical social reformers of the nineteenth century. He championed many causes during his lifetime, but is best known for his fight for the abolition of slavery. He is remembered in the lectionary on 30 July.

Wilberforce's crusade was inspired by strong evangelical belief. He was born in 1759 to wealthy parents in Hull. His father died when he was a child; the young William stayed with his aunt and uncle. His relatives, who were influenced by the early evangelical revival, were friends of John Newton. Newton, a former slave trader, was a rector in London and a writer of hymns.

William's mother took him away from this religious influence by sending him off to boarding school. From there he went to St John's College, Cambridge, and became friends with William Pitt (the younger). Both men wanted a political career. Wilberforce was recognized as an orator; at the age of 21 he became MP for Hull, and later for Yorkshire. Pitt was to become Prime Minister.

In 1785 Wilberforce travelled round Europe. Through reading the Bible and talking to friends he became convinced of the truth of the gospel. He went to see his relatives' friend John Newton, toying with the idea of giving up politics. Newton persuaded him to take up the cause of Christianity in Parliament.

Wilberforce became an influential Christian presence among those in power. He was convinced of his vocation to the great: 'There was needed some reformer of the nation's morals and who should raise his voice in the high places of the land.' He lived in Clapham and became a prominent member of the Clapham Sect, a group of influential evangelicals. He helped found many voluntary societies, including the Church Missionary Society (1798), the Bible Society (1803), and welfare societies for various disadvantaged groups.

But it was to the issue of slavery that Wilberforce devoted most of his energies and time. Through his Quaker friends and John Newton, Wilberforce was convinced of the evil of the trade. He made many enemies among those who benefited from it, but he was tireless in his campaign. He and his friends organized public meetings throughout the country, and published descriptions of the terrible conditions slaves suffered on the ships from Africa to America and the West Indies, and of their suffering in the plantations. The bill for the abolition of the trade finally became law in 1807. Wilberforce and his friends hoped that slavery would die once it was illegal to buy and sell slaves. But instead the slave trade went underground and continued. For another 26 years Wilberforce fought for the emancipation of slaves. In 1833, three days before he died, a law was passed to end slavery in all British possessions.

THEMES

If Wilberforce were around today he would still have work to do. **Slavery** is still with us, and Christians continue to campaign for its abolition. For children the work of Christian Aid highlighting the injustice of child labour in different countries provides an accessible way of looking at modern forms of slavery (Christian Aid, PO Box 100, SE1 7RT).

Slavery flourishes through greed and lack of compassion: its source, in other words, lies in human **sin**. That connection becomes all the more vivid if we see sin itself as a form of slavery from which people need to be released. St Paul, the first Christian theologian, explores this idea (Romans 6.16-20), which also appears in the Prayer over the Water in the baptism service.

> Through water you led the children of Israel from slavery in Egypt to freedom in the promised land.
> In water your Son Jesus received the baptism of John and was anointed by the Holy Spirit as the Messiah, the Christ,
> to lead us from the death of sin to newness of life.
>
> *Holy Baptism Service, Common Worship: Initiation Services*

Easter occupies a position in the Christian faith comparable to the Passover in Judaism, indeed Easter is the Christian Passover: deliverance from slavery in Egypt becomes the metaphor for deliverance from sin achieved by Christ's death and resurrection. Every individual human being is involved in the sin that characterizes the human race. On the cross Christ conquers sin; in baptism the individual is delivered from the slavery of sin and becomes obedient to God.

Timing

The Bible study and song can be combined with the chain activity to form a whole session. The campaigning activity can take up to a whole session.

Activities

Bible study and song – for all ages

The story of the plagues of Egypt and of Moses' appeals to Pharoah to 'let my people go' occupies fourteen chapters of the book of Exodus (3–16), too big a 'chunk' to swallow in one session. However the story is very graphic, can be found in many simplified versions, and lends itself well to adaptation by the gifted story-teller. Older children will enjoy reading it, especially in the 'dramatized Bible' version. However, time commitments will probably require an outline story of the conditions of slavery in Egypt, the plagues and the pleadings, followed by closer attention to chapter 14. This story speaks of a God who wants people to be free, and who has active involvement in human history.

The story of the Exodus (which comes from the Greek for 'the way out') was taken up by the very slaves for whose freedom Wilberforce campaigned. The story strengthened their faith and gave them hope of freedom. Their rich tradition of 'spirituals' contains many references to Exodus. Explain this to the children, then sing 'When Israel was in Egypt's land' using appropriate actions.

Chained together – for older children

Both slavery and sin hold human beings captive and limit their freedom. To stop them from escaping, slaves were often chained together. This activity 'chains' children in pairs and brings their release.

METHOD

- One child passes their hands into the loops as if they were wearing handcuffs.
- The other child puts one hand into a loop of the other rope, passes the rope

You will need

two lengths of rope approximately 1 m in length with a loop at either end large enough for a hand to go through.

When Israel was in Egypt's land

Afro-American Spiritual

2 The Lord told Moses what to do,
   let my people go,
   to lead the children of Israel through,
   let my people go.

3 Your foes shall not before you stand,
   let my people go,
   and you'll possess fair Canaan's land,
   let my people go.

4 O let us all from bondage flee,
   let my people go,
   and let all in Christ be free,
   let my people go.

5 I do believe without a doubt,
   let my people go,
   a Christian has a right to shout,
   let my people go.

round the 'handcuff' rope then puts their other hand through the loop.

- Now discuss with the children the experience of being 'chained' together: it means restriction of movement, lack of space, mobility etc.
- Now ask them to get out of the link without pulling their hands out of the loops. The children will probably have so much fun doing this that the wrong message might be given about sin! Nevertheless, frustration usually takes over.
- Then say that we are all bound together in human sin. To be free we need Jesus Christ.
- Now tell them how to escape. In a similar way, listening to the word of God in Scripture allows us to be rescued from sin and to live in freedom.
- To escape one person makes a large loop using most of the length of their rope. This loop is then passed inside one of the 'bracelets' of the other person and over their hand. The rope can now be removed and the pair are separated.

Campaigning – for older children

William Wilberforce believed that he could change injustice through politics and political action. Using materials from Christian Aid and other agencies encourage the children to prepare a 'soap box' speech on why slavery or child labour must be stopped. They can pretend that they are William Wilberforce campaigning to stop slavery in the last century or they can be a modern politician fighting against child labour today. Discuss the importance of making their speech short, clear, direct and hard hitting. The group can then take it in turns to deliver their message on a 'soap box'.

If younger children want to join in a similar activity they can make simple rosettes, like party political rosettes, or badges which state 'Fight Slavery'.

Maximilian Kolbe

Martyrdom in Auschwitz

*Maximilian
Kolbe
Photo:
The Catholic
Truth Society*

Auschwitz – the very word still carries the chill horror of the atrocities inflicted there. Maximilian Kolbe, a Polish Franciscan friar and, to the Nazis, a dangerous journalist, was arrested in Warsaw in February 1941 and transferred to Auschwitz in May. The regime in the concentration camp decreed that, in the event of one prisoner escaping, ten were sentenced to death. Following an escape in July 1941, men from Kolbe's block were paraded for selection to be executed. An army sergeant, Francis Gajowniczek, was called out, but

Kolbe stepped forward and volunteered to take his place. The sergeant had a wife and children, whereas he was – in his own words – 'an old man' with no dependants. He was 47. So Kolbe was locked up and starved for two weeks, during which time he encouraged his fellow condemned prisoners by his prayers and hymn singing. Only four survived the starvation, including Kolbe. He, like them, was given a lethal injection and died on 14 August, the eve of the Feast of the Assumption.

Kolbe's hope, expressed to his friends, had always been that he might die on a feast of Our Lady because he had a special devotion to her. At the age of ten he had a vision of Mary offering him two crowns, one white, one red. Some thirteen years later, while studying in Rome, he started a 'Militia of Mary Immaculate' to promote devotion to Mary. Having read philosophy with the Jesuits and theology with the Franciscans, Kolbe became a Franciscan, taking the name Maximilian (he had been baptized Raymund) and was ordained as a priest. He returned to Poland in 1919, but poor health initially hampered his work with the Militia. However, he recovered and set about his task with renewed energy. He set up many groups, maintaining their unity by means of a periodical, *The Knight of the Immaculate*, which he also used to attract new recruits. His phenomenal success speaks for itself – a quarter of a million Poles had joined the Militia by the late 1920s.

Then Kolbe started a new venture: Niepokalanow, 'City of Mary', was a Franciscan friary outside Warsaw which expanded in the ten years from its foundation to the start of the second World War to accommodate 800 friars. It produced no fewer than eleven publications, one of them a daily newspaper. And as the original 'City of Mary' grew, Kolbe set off to spread further the devotion to Mary. Within a month of his arrival in Japan the first Japanese edition of *The Knight* appeared. From there he went to India to establish more 'cities of Mary', before being recalled to lead the original Polish foundation. It was while engaged on this work that Kolbe was arrested and his final imprisonment began.

The story of Maximilian Kolbe's death reveals reason enough to declare him a saint. But the story of his life is equally eloquent testimony to the depth of his faith. The Pope canonized him on 10 October 1982.

THEMES

Such an active and varied life as Kolbe's is rich in themes and examples for others to follow: the sheer energy and strength of his faith; his use of newspapers and publications to disseminate that faith; his establishing of Franciscan institutions; his vision and inner spiritual experience; his tireless mission to the whole world; above all perhaps his willingness to live out Christ's words 'greater love has no-one than this, that he lay down his life for his friends' (John 15.13). The ideas here focus on his **martyrdom** and on his use of the **printed word**.

TIMING

Each of these activities can take one session.

Activity ideas
The martyr's crown – for younger children

Tell the story of Kolbe's vision and of his final months and death. Explain that in the history of the Church we sometimes speak of 'red' martyrs or witnesses and 'white' martyrs. The former are those people who love and follow Jesus and who are killed for their faith by wicked people; the latter are those who are not killed, but whose whole life is specially dedicated to the service of God and of others. Most Christians do not have to die for their beliefs, but we are to live for God and for others. This activity links those two forms of martyrdom.

METHOD
- Explain that the friar represents Maximilian Kolbe.
- On the back of the template let the children either stick a photograph of themselves or draw a picture of themselves.
- Ask each child to colour one half of the crown in red and fold it in two.
- Glue the crown to the top of the friar figure. The red crown for Kolbe and the white crown for the child are a sign that every Christian is called to give their life in God's service.

Read all about it – for older children

Tell the children the story of Maximilian Kolbe and get the group to talk about it. In particular focus on his martyrdom: why did he act as he did? Would they have done the same? What do his actions tell us about his faith? Make the connection between Kolbe's actions and Jesus' words about laying down one's life for one's friends.

Now let the children, alone or in groups, produce a special edition of *The Knight of the Immaculate*. Let them design a heading using motifs from the story (red and white crowns, Our Lady) and get them to report the story of Maximilian Kolbe in their own words and drawings. If you have ready access to a photocopier you could print enough copies for the whole congregation. Let the children then distribute their paper as Kolbe distributed his.

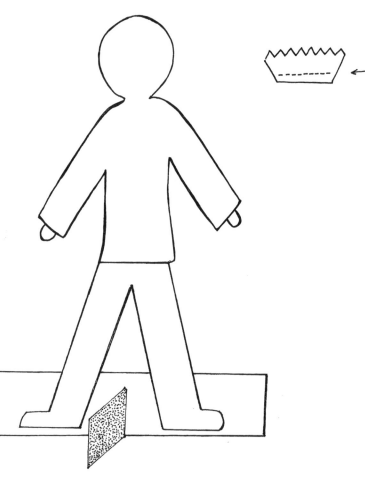

You will need for each child

a template figure of a Franciscan friar

a photograph of each child (or get them to draw themselves)

drawing materials

a crown template, hinged in the middle

glue

← cut

You will need

paper

drawing materials

scissors

glue

William and Catherine Booth

Founders of the Salvation Army

William and
Catherine Booth
Photo: *The
Salvation Army
International
Heritage Centre*

Of all the revivalist movements in modern times, the Salvation Army ranks as one of the most successful. The vision of its founders, William and Catherine Booth, still inspires people today, whether or not they share the faith of those who commit their lives to service in the Army. Born in Nottingham in 1827, partly of Jewish stock, William Booth became a Methodist minister and a passionate evangelist. In 1861, fifteen years after he began his preaching career, Booth parted company with the Methodists, who had wanted him to moderate his sometimes violent style of proclaiming the word of God. He established in Whitechapel in London his 'Christian Mission', which already showed the features by which the Salvation Army is recognized today – at the centre a strong emphasis on evangelistic preaching together with a strong commitment to social and rescue work. The Mission reflects the man, who had a deep love of the poor which inspired him to care for them physically and to provide nurture for their souls to bring them to salvation. In his work William Booth had the staunch support of his wife Catherine, who was a powerful preacher in her own right. She also spoke to people in their homes and to alcoholics whom she helped to make a new start in life. She also spoke to the wealthy, gaining financial support for the Army's work. Booth died in 1912, and William's son William Bramwell Booth suceeded him as General.

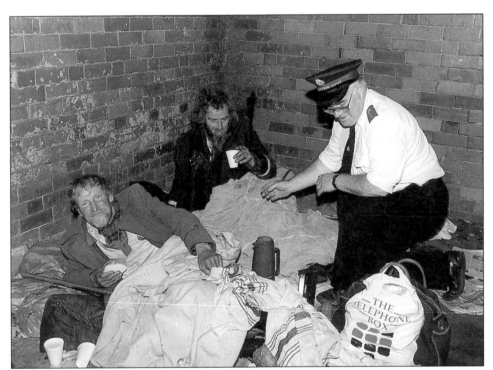

Photo: *The Salvation Army*

THEMES

Today's Salvation Army is instantly recognized all over the world: the uniform, the band, the *War Cry* newspaper, the soup kitchens, the service to the most needy people. There is therefore a wealth of themes. These suggestions focus on just three. **Good News to the Poor** – the members of the Salvation Army are a familiar sight in the pubs selling their newspaper the *War Cry*', taking **good news** into unlikely places and sharing it with people who might well resist. The children can seek out in the wordsearch provided the different groups of people whom the Salvation Army helps today. The bands embody the strong **music tradition** of the

Salvation Army. The children can learn a simple rap. The soup kitchens are associated with the Salvation Army. It would be impractical for children to set up a **soup kitchen** among the homeless, but they could make soup and hand it out to the congregation or to their friends to remind them that before God we all have the same status, rich or poor. The recipients might also be encouraged to make a donation to diminish the gap!

TIMING

The wordsearch will only take a few minutes. The rap will take part of a session and the cooking a whole session. Please ensure that there is sufficient adult supervision for the cooking activity.

Activity ideas
'Seeking out the poor' wordsearch – for all ages

Encourage the children to find out more about the Salvation Army's work amongst the homeless, the elderly, prisoners, the addicted, the disabled, young people and the needy. Education packs are available from the Salvation Army, 101 Queen Victoria Street, London EC4P 4EP. If possible invite a Salvation Army Officer to the group to talk about their work and beliefs.

In this wordsearch, shaped like a Salvation Army flag, you have to seek out those people whom Jesus sought out during his lifetime – the outcast, the leper, the sick and needy; and also those whom the Salvation Army seek out today: addicts, the homeless. Among all these needy people you will also find Jesus himself.

Seeking out the poor

In this wordsearch, shaped like a Salvation Army flag, you have to seek out those people whom Jesus sought out during his lifetime – the outcast, the leper, the sick and needy – and also those whom the Salvation Army seek out today – addicts and the homeless. Among all these needy people, you will also find Jesus himself.

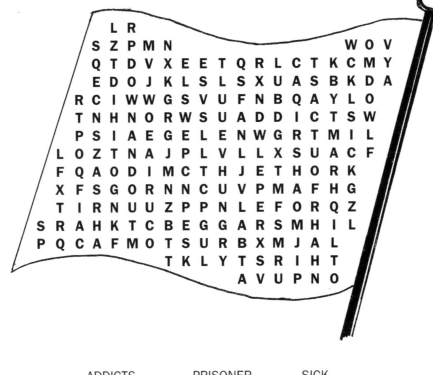

```
      L R
    S Z P M N                       W O V
    Q T D V X E E T Q R L C T K C M Y
    E D O J K L S L S X U A S B K D A
  R C I W W G S V U F N B Q A Y L O
  T N H N O R W S U A D D I C T S W
  P S I A E G E L E N W G R T M I L
L O Z T N A J P L V L L X S U A C F
F Q A O D I M C T H J E T H O R K
X F S G O R N N C U V P M A F H G
T I R N U U Z P P N L E F O R Q Z
S R A H K T C B E G G A R S M H I L
P Q C A F M O T S U R B X M J A L
        T K L Y T S R I H T
          A V U P N O
```

ADDICTS	PRISONER	SICK
HOMELESS	NEEDY	OUTCAST
DOWNANDOUT	THIRSTY	
BEGGARS	LEPER	JESUS
HUNGRY	UNCLEAN	

Making music for God – a rap for all ages

From the early days of the movement Salvationists have held meetings in the streets so that the Christian message would reach those who do not go to church. They have also always used music to help them pass on the Christian message. The early brass bands had a double purpose – in providing a good accompaniment to the singing and in drowning out the noise of hecklers. William Booth appreciated the usefulness of adapting familiar melodies from the music hall with a Christian text so 'Champagne Charlie is my name' became 'Bless his name he sets me free'. Today this tradition continues and Salvation Army worship includes the music and rhythm of the modern world. The children can learn this simple rap which is sometimes used by the Salvation Army in their more informal worship.

Rapazac (rap style)

There was a man named Zac from Jericho,
He wasn't very big but he had a lot of dough
Did Zac (Rapazac), did Zac (Rapazac).

The people didn't like him and that's a fact,
He did a lot of this (*grabbing money action*), and an
awful lot of that (*hands in pocket action*)
Did Zac (Rapazac), did Zac (Rapazac).

Now Zacchaeus changed because of that tea,
He gave away his goods to charity.

Now Zac was changed and his family too,
they all became saved and so can you -
Like Zac (Rapazac), like Zac (Rapazac).

Making soup – for older children

Every year, the Salvation Army in the UK provides more than a million subsidized meals for the elderly, and more than four and a half million meals for the homeless and needy. Every night it houses around 5,000 people. Throughout the country it is known for its work in providing soup and other food for the homeless. Children can make this simple soup to serve after a service to members of the congregation or class. They can ask for a donation towards the work of the Salvation Army.

This recipe provides enough soup for up to fifteen people. Please adjust the measurements accordingly to make larger quantities. Ensure that there is sufficient adult supervision for the cutting and cooking required.

METHOD

- Chop up all the vegetables into small pieces.
- Heat the oil in a large saucepan and add the chopped onion. Fry until it is translucent.
- Add all the other vegetables, pasta, stock, chopped parsley and seasoning and bring to the boil.
- Simmer for around twenty minutes or until all the vegetables are cooked.
- Serve in warmed bowls with the bread rolls.

You will need

a hob or gas ring

aprons

knives

chopping board

a very large saucepan

bowls and spoons to serve

bread rolls

three onions

three table-spoons of cooking oil

750 g chopped root vegetables

750 g chopped green vegetables

100 g pasta shapes

three table-spoons of chopped parsley

two litres of stock

seasoning

The Blessed Virgin Mary

Mary, Mother of Jesus *by Raffaello d'Urbino* Photo: *Mary Evans Picture Library*

Joseph, son of David, do not fear to take Mary your wife, for that which is conceived in her is of the Holy Spirit; she will bear a son, and you shall call his name Jesus, for he will save his people from their sins. (Matthew 1.20)

Matthew's famous words summarize the events which Luke describes in greater detail – the visit of the Angel Gabriel to announce to Mary that she will conceive a child by the Holy Spirit; her obedient response, 'Behold, I am the handmaid of the Lord; let it be to me according to your word'

(Luke 1.38). Soon follows the visit to Elizabeth, during which Mary praises God in words which the Church has echoed all down the centuries and still sings today, 'My soul doth magnify the Lord'. As the mother of Jesus, Mary is the first to worship him and to welcome others into the fellowship of praise – shepherds and Magi alike. She is also the first to share in his sorrows. When she and Joseph take the one-week-old Jesus to the Temple for purification, the old prophet Simeon tells them:

> Behold, this child is set for the fall and rising of many in Israel, and for a sign
> that is spoken against (and a sword will pierce through your own soul also),
> that thoughts out of many hearts may be revealed. (Luke 2.34-35)

Though she fades into the background during Jesus' adult ministry, she experiences the pain of that sword as she watches her son die on the cross. There, in his final agony, Jesus binds her in mutual care with the beloved disciple (John 19.26). And she continues with Jesus' friends, for she is numbered among those who frequently prayed with the disciples in Acts 1 and 2, upon whom the Holy Spirit came at Pentecost.

As well as bearing Jesus, Mary embodies many of those virtues which we recognize as Christ-like: obedience to God, humility, faithfulness, love stronger than death, compassion, a rejection of the worldly values that elevate one at the expense of another. The events of her life and the qualities of her character have exercised an irresistible fascination for disciples, theologians, artists and musicians. She is depicted in her tender humanity as she cradles the infant Jesus or with equal tenderness holds the broken crucified body in her arms; or she is shown in regal state with crown and sceptre; or she is portrayed in her strength. In all these respects we see reflected through Mary the glory of God himself, and it is above all for this reason that she is held in such veneration.

THEMES

In art many of Mary's virtues are represented **symbolically** – the lily for purity, her blue robe showing her election by God. The title 'Star of the sea' (*Stella Maris*) goes back to the fourth century: St Jerome interpreted the Hebrew version of Mary (Miryam) as meaning 'Star of the Sea', a title which frequently occurs in hymns. The hymn 'Crown Him with Many Crowns' shows another symbolic title 'Mystic Rose', which dates from the Middle Ages. The hymn uses the image to show that Christ is both born of Mary and also the divine principle through which she, like the rest of the created order, came to be – Christ is both 'fruit' and 'stem' of the rose. The 'Mystic Rose' points to her special position ('highly favoured') and her common humanity. The **monogram** is not strictly a symbol, rather a visual representation for Mary. It incorporates in one simple device all five letters of her name in Latin (Maria) and is frequently found in architectural decoration, banners and other art forms. These activities explore these symbols and the monogram.

TIMING

Each of these activities can take one session.

Activity ideas

A concertina book of Mary's life – for all ages

Talk with the group about Mary's life and the different events she experienced.

METHOD

Using the biblical references given in the opening paragraph of this chapter, ask the children to draw their own book of Mary's life making each event a picture on a separate page.

Mary's monogram – for all ages

Talk with the group about different logos or monograms that they know today – MacDonalds, Bhs, WH Smith etc. Explain to the group that in a pre-literate age, Mary's monogram illustrated here would be immediately recognizable by people even though they might not be able to read. Encourage the group to design their own monogram incorporating all the letters of their name. The monogram can then be drawn on a card or a badge.

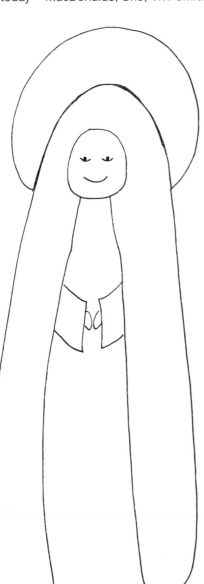

A Mary peg doll – for older children

Discuss the different symbols for Mary with the group. If possible take in pictures from art books to illustrate your points. Talk about the type of woman they think Mary was. How would they illustrate her?

They can then make a peg doll of Mary holding one of the symbols described in the introduction or one they believe illustrates something about her nature.

METHOD

- Attach a pipe-cleaner around the body of the peg to make the 'arms'.
- Using remnants of cloth make appropriate clothes for the figure of Mary and sew them in place.
- With felt-tip pens draw facial features.
- Draw and cut out the symbol chosen and attach to the pipe-cleaner hands of the figure.

St Ninian

Bishop of Galloway, Apostle to the Picts

Whithorn crosses now housed in the Whithorn Museum Photo: Historic Scotland

Ninian is believed to have been born in the year AD 360 into a Christian family in Cumbria where his father was a chieftain or king. Bede's *A History of the English Church and People* is the main source for information on St Ninian. From Bede we learn that Ninian was a holy man of British race who converted the southern Picts. Bede also writes that Ninian received his instruction in Rome and that his church was dedicated to St Martin. The church was known as the *Candida Casa* (White House) and it was built in a style unfamiliar to the Britons at that time.

Seven centuries after Ninian's death, in the twelfth century, Ailred of Rievaulx also wrote a Life of this popular saint. Ailred's Life, based on an earlier, now lost Anglo-Saxon account, contains many of the great legends associated with Ninian. Ailred writes that Ninian was befriended by the Pope when he was in Rome and after many years there he was consecrated as bishop and sent home. On the way back he passed through Gaul (France) and stayed with St Martin in Tours. When he finally reached home he settled in Whithorn in Galloway where he founded an abbey, the *Candida Casa*. It was built by masons Ninian had brought from Gaul. Whithorn was his base for many missionary journeys throughout Cumbria. Place names and archaeological finds testify to his influence in the area. Ninian then began missionary work amongst the Picts. He is believed to have worked along the north-east coast of Scotland and further north. Two centuries later St Columba was to begin evangelizing amongst the northern Picts.

THEMES

Protection – many legends and stories of miracles grew up about Ninian and how he was able to protect people and animals. The Celtic idea of a circle of protection and 'caim prayers' are explored here.

Building up the Church – Ninian is remembered as the person who brought the gospel to the southern Picts. He did this from his base at the church in Whithorn. This church was remarkable because it was built from stones rather than mud and thatch and by masons from Gaul. Whithorn became an important monastic settlement and ruins of a church and monastery there remain. The spread of the Christian Church in the region is also shown by the large inscribed stone crosses in the area. But the Church is not just bricks and mortar or stones but the people. It was the 'living stones' who Ninian converted who helped build up the Church in the area. The theme of '**living stones**' is explored here.

TIMING

The circle of protection and cross pendant each take a session.

Activity ideas
A circle of protection – for all ages

Many stories and legends about Ninian survive. Although their historical accuracy may be in doubt, all aim to show that Ninian was a holy man who followed Christ in all he did. One legend recounted in Ailred's Life tells how Ninian used to visit his shepherds, flocks and herds. One night when the shepherds and Ninian were ready to go to bed, Ninian gathered the animals together and walked in a circle around them, commanding that all within the circle should be under God's protection that night. During the night, while they were sleeping, thieves came to the place. As they could see no walls, hedges or ditches to stop them they tried to steal the cattle. But they were unsuccessful. The bull of the herd attacked the leader of the thieves and killed him. When Ninian awoke and saw what had happened he prayed that the man might be saved. The thief was miraculously raised from death. The other thieves were imprisoned by 'a certain madness within the circle which the saint had made'. Trapped and helpless they appealed to Ninian to save them. Ninian spoke to them of God, blessed them and let them go free.

For the Celtic people God was immediate and involved in their everyday activity. His care and protection was described in very immediate and concrete terms. In the story of St Ninian's cattle recounted here we see the common Celtic idea of God's protection being like a circle encompassing all that is to be protected. These ideas give rise to **caim prayers**, in which Celtic Christians extended the forefinger of the right hand and drew an imaginary circle around themselves asking for protection. This can be a helpful image to explore with children. They cannot see God, his protection is not like a security fence or a locked door but it is nevertheless there.

This prayer by David Adam appears in *The Edge of Glory*:

Circle me Lord
Keep protection near
And danger afar.

Circle me Lord
Keep hope within
Keep doubt without.

Circle me Lord
Keep light near
And darkness afar.

Circle me Lord
Keep peace within
Keep evil out.

Make sufficient copies of the template of a Celtic circle above. Ask the children to use the first line of David Adam's poem to write their own prayer asking for God's protection. Younger children could draw a picture of themselves inside the circle and outside pictures of things they are afraid of.

Once completed the prayer pictures could form part of an act of worship. The children might draw an imaginary circle around themselves with their hands as they say their prayer or stand in a circle as a group.

Living stones:
Whithorn cross pendants – for all ages

In Bede Ninian is the saint who is remembered for building the 'White House' and this site is now a site of great archaeological interest. Whithorn is the scene of the earliest recorded Christian mission in Scotland and became an important monastery. Throughout the Whithorn area in Galloway there are distinctive stone crosses which are known as the Whithorn crosses. Although most of these date from a later period than Ninian they serve as a reminder of the witness of the saint and his influence in the area. These crosses are believed to have been erected to commemorate priests and chieftains and probably originally stood on their graves. They might have stood in Christian cemeteries or on sites set apart for services held in the open. The crosses have a distinctive shape. They are flat shafts of stone with circular heads like that illustrated on page 83.

Children often think of the Church as a building, a construction of stones, like Ninian's first church, but it is important that they also appreciate that the Church is people, 'living stones' who like Ninian show people about Jesus through their lives. With older children you could explore the theme of living stones from 1 Peter 2.4. 'Come to the Lord, the living stone rejected by people as worthless but chosen by God as valuable. Come as living stones, and let yourselves be used in building the spiritual temple . . .' (GNB).

The Whithorn crosses remind people that Ninian's influence was great. Many heard about the story of Jesus through Ninian's followers. These may have been chieftains or priests whose graves are marked by the stone crosses or those who prayed in the open air at the site of the crosses. The buildings and stones are both important but it was the saint and his followers who brought the Christian faith to the people of the area. It was the 'living stones' who provided the Christian heritage and the buildings and stones which remain remind people of this heritage. The children can make their own Whithorn cross pendants to wear as a reminder that they too are the Church, the 'living stones'.

METHOD

- Give a small lump of clay the size of a walnut to each child and ask them to follow these instructions.
- Mould the lump into a smooth ball without any cracks in.
- Flatten the balls to create a disc shape.
- Insert a paper clip carefully into one end of the disc in the middle of the clay and press into shape again.
- With a pen top carefully press the disc with the five circles as shown in the illustration. Younger children can make a simple cross shape in their clay stamping out a cross shape with the pen tops.
- Carefully press out the rest of the cross shape as shown with a knife.
- Attach a length of string and tie it to make a pendant.
- Leave the models to dry.

You will need

a packet of modelling clay – the type that dries hard when left uncovered

pen and pencil tops

knives

paper clips

table coverings

string

St Luke

The medicine of the Gospel

Return of the Prodigal Son *by Harmensz van Rijan Rembrandt (1906–69). Hermitage,St. Petersburg* Photo: *Bridgeman Art Library, London/New York*

St Luke belongs to that small number of people in any given age who make outstanding contributions to a number of different areas of life. First and foremost of course he is celebrated as one of the four evangelists upon whom we depend for our knowledge of Jesus. His Gospel record emphasizes the warmth, humanity and sociability of Jesus and is treasured for the parables not found elsewhere, notably the Good Samaritan and the Prodigal Son. The settings in which Luke describes Jesus are often homely, involving a meal shared among friends. It is typical of Luke that he records the story of the risen Jesus walking along the road to Emmaus with two friends, going into their home for supper and making himself known in the breaking of bread. Some commentators suggest that these friends were man and wife, and this too would fit with Luke's account of Jesus including men and women, often by telling two similar stories in which the main characters are male and female respectively.

In his Gospel, Luke presents an 'orderly account' of part one of the history he charts; part two follows in the book of Acts, which Luke also wrote. As well as being an evangelist, Luke is therefore also rightly considered an historian, with a distinctive understanding of Jesus Christ standing in the middle of human history. To his contemporaries, however, Luke was not noted either as evangelist or historian. Paul calls him 'the beloved physician', and given Paul's repeated references to his own poor health, we can take it he knew what he was talking about. Luke accompanied Paul in his travels, thus adding the role of missionary to his many accomplishments. As if all this were not enough, tradition maintains that he painted a portrait of the Virgin Mary, so his patronage, which includes the medical profession, also extends to include various kinds of artistic activity.

THEMES

'Repentance and forgiveness of sins is to be proclaimed in Christ's name to all nations, beginning from Jerusalem' (Luke 24.47, NRSV). As Jesus spoke, so Luke acted. He himself was involved in the earliest **missionary work** of the Church, which he chronicled in Acts. The 'To All Nations' board game teaches some of the joys and troubles of those first Christians. The second activity focuses on a parable peculiar to Luke – the '**Prodigal Son**'.

TIMING

The board game may take more than one session. It will take one session to make the finger puppets and do a simple drama.

Activity ideas
'To All Nations' board game – for all ages

Proclaiming the gospel to all nations from Jerusalem is the theme of this simple board game. Just as the first disciples and missionaries of the Church faced hardships and danger as well as encouragements in preaching the gospel in all four corners of the known world, so will the players of this game face setbacks and receive help in their game. The game can be adapted in different ways but needs to be made and played by four players.

You will need

a large sheet of card

drawing materials

four counters

a ruler

dice

METHOD

- Divide the sheet into four as shown and mark out the same number of squares in each of the four sections.
- Over the four central squares write in 'Jerusalem' and decorate appropriately.
- In each of the four corners of the board write 'North', 'South', 'East' and 'West'.
- Number each section's squares.
- Using the hardships and encouragements given on the next page write appropriate instructions on different squares – e.g. Peter and John jailed, move back 5; filled with the Holy Spirit, move on 4. Give each section more encouragements than hardships and add to the list given by reading on from chapter 16 of the Acts of the Apostles. The number of spaces they move forward and backward on each instruction will depend on the number of squares in the section.
- The four players can now play the game by taking it in turns to throw the dice. Each player chooses one section and moves within that section. This is not a game of winners or losers. The gospel message is only passed on when all four players reach their destination.

North		53	52	51	50	49	48	48	49	50	51	52	53	East	
40	41	42	43	44	45	46	47	47	46	45	44	43	42	41	40
39	38	37	36	35	34	33	32	32	33	34	35	36	37	38	39
24	25	26	27	28	29	30	31	31	30	29	28	27	26	25	24
23	22	21	20	19	18	17	16	16	17	18	19	20	21	22	23
8	9	10	11	12	13	14	15	15	14	13	12	11	10	9	8
7	6	5	4	3	2	1	**Jerusalem**	1	2	3	4	5	6	7	
7	6	5	4	3	2	1		1	2	3	4	5	6	7	
8	9	10	11	12	13	14	15	15	14	13	12	11	10	9	8
23	22	21	20	19	18	17	16	16	17	18	19	20	21	22	23
24	25	26	27	28	29	30	31	31	30	29	28	27	26	25	24
39	38	37	36	35	34	33	32	32	33	34	35	36	37	38	39
40	41	42	43	44	45	46	47	47	46	45	44	43	42	41	40
West		53	52	51	50	49	48	48	49	50	51	52	53	South	

Hardships:
- Peter and John jailed (Acts 4.3);
- Stephen stoned to death (Acts 7.58);
- Persecution of the Church (Acts 8.1);
- King Herod kills James (Acts 12.2);
- Flee Iconium (Acts 14.6);
- Paul and Silas jailed (Acts 16.24).

Encouragements:
- Filled with the Holy Spirit (Acts 2.4);
- Three thousand baptized (Acts 2.41);
- Lame man cured (Acts 3.7);
- Angel opens prison doors (Acts 5.19);
- Ethiopian baptized (Acts 8.38);
- Conversion of Saul (Acts 9);
- Dorcas raised from dead (Acts 9.41);
- Gospel is for all people (Acts 10.34ff);
- Prison chains fall off (Acts 12.7).

Finger puppets – for all ages

Read the story of the Prodigal Son with the group (Luke 15.11ff.) and talk with them about the different characters in the story. Discuss the following questions with them to get them thinking about a drama.

- What do they think about the younger son who asks for his inheritance?
- How would they have felt if they were the father?
- How would they have felt if they were the older son?
- What do they think the younger son felt like when he was cleaning out the pigs?
- If they were the father would they have forgiven the younger son when he returned home?
- Would they have been jealous like the older son?

They can then make these simple finger puppets out of card and act out the play themselves. They can either do this in pairs or in a larger group.

METHOD

- Cut out and colour each of the figures.
- Make into a finger puppet by making a loop with the bottom tabs and securing with sticky tape.

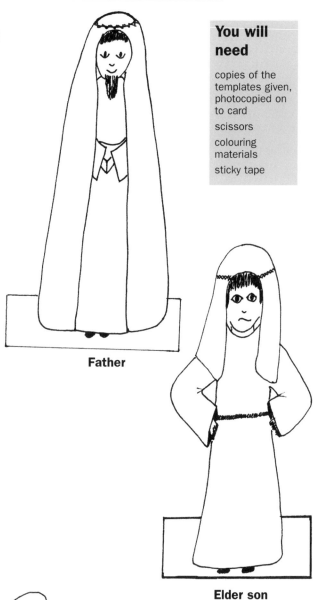

Father

You will need

copies of the templates given, photocopied on to card

scissors

colouring materials

sticky tape

Elder son

Cut three pigs

Pig farmer

Younger son

Alfred the Great

King and scholar

Alfred, King of the West Saxons. *Anon. engraving* Photo: *Mary Evans Picture Library*

Alfred lived in turbulent times. Ninth-century England consisted of separate kingdoms which had – with one exception – been brutally conquered by the ruthless Vikings. The exception was Wessex, Alfred's kingdom. In 878 a new Viking army led by Guthrum launched a surprise attack on Wessex, conquering most of it. But Alfred withdrew to plan a fightback. Having gathered an army together, he attacked and defeated Guthrum. The Vikings were driven back to the north and east coast of England. Alfred refused to make peace unless the Vikings accepted the Christian faith. Along with 29 other chiefs, Guthrum was baptized, with Alfred himself as godfather. Alfred then allowed them to settle in peace in East Anglia. Alfred consolidated support in the rest of England and Wales and laid the foundation for a united kingdom. Not for nothing was he called 'great' – the only English king to be so recognized.

Yet for all his courage and skill as a soldier, success in conflict was only one of his attributes. Alfred was a deeply religious man who lived by the Golden Rule 'Do unto others as you would they should do unto you' (based on Matthew 7.12). He was able to make peace as well as war, establishing just laws based on the ten commandments. Having learned to read at the age of 38 he became a man of culture and learning, translating Latin books into his native English. He was a generous benefactor, spending half of the kingdom's money on restoring and building monasteries and churches, on education and on provision for the poor. He gained the devotion of his compatriots and the respect and trust of the Viking settlers. On one famous occasion when he was wronged by a Viking leader, Alfred took his wife and children hostage. The Vikings would have expected them to be killed, but Alfred sent them home again, bearing gifts, because mercy is required of a Christian ruler. Alfred died in 902 at the age of 53.

THEMES

Alfred's rich history contains many treasures. Reading, education and **scholarship** were of passionate concern to him. The 'Alfred Jewel' bookmark highlights this aspect of his life. Alfred established peace and ruled his kingdom with justice. He treated even his enemies according to the **Golden Rule**, showing that justice alone falls short of what is required of a Christian: mercy is needed too. The framed mirror in which we see ourselves reinforces this Golden Rule. The scales of justice extend the idea to more particular qualities which we must have if we are to treat others as we would want them to treat us.

TIMING

The Alfred Jewel colouring need not take long. The mirror and scales will each take one session.

Activity ideas

An Alfred jewel bookmark – for younger children

King Alfred was a passionate believer in the importance of education, although he only learnt to read and write when he was 38. Later he translated books from Latin into English including a book by Pope Gregory the Great. He made sure that every bishop in the country received a copy of this book. This is the Alfred Jewel which might be a marker Alfred sent with the book to a bishop. On the side of the jewel it says 'Alfred ordered me to be made'. Today the Alfred Jewel is in the Ashmolean Museum in Oxford. Children can colour in copies of the template of the jewel and use them as bookmarks as a reminder of Alfred's love of books.

You will need

a copy of the template for each child

colouring materials

A Golden Rule mirror – for older children

Alfred's Golden Rule was 'Do unto others as you would they should do unto you'. Talk with the group about whether they ever make rules up for themselves or make New Year resolutions. Or do they have a motto which they try to apply in their lives – 'I will try to help at home once a day', 'I will try to be nice to my friends', etc. Discuss what might be an appropriate motto for them as followers of Jesus. They can then incorporate their motto into the mirror design so that every time they look at themselves they are reminded of their own Golden Rule.

METHOD

*   In the centre of the card draw the shape of the mirror, but 1 cm smaller all the way around. Cut out this shape.
*   Ask each child to write their Golden Rule on a sticky label and place on the card border.
*   Using a length of string coil spirals and swirls around the border and secure in place with PVA glue.

You will need

a small mirror for each child or a piece of foil

a rectangle of thick card

PVA glue

scissors

ruler

string

sticky fixer pads

sticky labels

gold paint

drawing materials

- Allow the string to dry and then paint the frame and string, excluding the sticky label, with gold paint.
- Stick the mirror behind the opening using the sticky fixer pads. Alternatively stick a piece of foil behind the opening.
- Ask the children to prop their mirrors up against a wall or shelf at home and every time they look in it they can be reminded of their Golden Rule.

Scales of justice – for younger children

Alfred was a just king: not only did he keep his own Golden Rule but he showed the importance of justice in his kingdom. For younger children justice can be explained as fairness. In order that people have to be fair to them they need to be fair to those people, etc. The simple scales of justice remind them of Alfred's Golden Rule.

METHOD

- Cut two equal lengths of string and tie each around the empty yogurt pots.
- Hang the yogurt pots from each end of the coat-hanger.
- Ask the children to write the following words on sticky labels which they then stick on to the various coins. They should write the same sticky label for two matching coins – fair, kind, loving, loyal, helpful, good, etc.
- They can then hang their coat-hanger scales. If they put a coin in one yogurt pot scale they have to put the same-sized coin in the other side in order for the 'scales of justice' to balance.

You will need

a wire coat-hanger for each child

two empty yogurt pots for each child

a set of 1p, 2p, 5p, 10p and 50p coins

a set of sticky labels which will fit on all the coins

string

scissors

All Saints

A carousel of saints

The glorious company of apostles praise you: the noble fellowship of prophets praise you, the white-robed army of martyrs praise you. Throughout the world the holy Church acclaims you, Father of majesty unbounded.' The Te Deum gathers up our human songs of praise and joins our voices with those who have gone before us in the faith. All Saints is the season for special rejoicing in that great company. Many of them are known by name and have special days set aside for their commemoration: others are not known, or rather are known only to God. So this great festival serves to remind us that the treasures of the Christian tradition are richer than we can tell, and that our gratitude for all that we have received from other Christians is a debt that we can never fully pay. In our prayers at All Saints' Tide we reflect that this is true of the past as it is true also for the present: we receive from others more than we know or acknowledge, and our tendency is always to take one another for granted. In this season we remember that the biblical use of the word 'saint' is not restricted to those who have been formally canonized: all Christians are saints, and we all belong to that 'one communion and fellowship in the mystical body' of Christ (see the Collect for All Saints' Day below). This is a time therefore for celebration, for giving thanks for the number, variety and diversity of saints and for our unity in their company.

Collect

Almighty God,
you have knit together your elect
in one communion and fellowship
in the mystical body of your Son Christ our Lord:
grant us grace so to follow your blessed saints
in all virtuous and godly living
that we may come to those inexpressible joys
that you have prepared for those who truly love you;
through Jesus Christ your Son our Lord,
who is alive and reigns with you,
in the unity of the Holy Spirit,
one God, now and for ever.

Collect for All Saints' Day in *The Christian Year: Calendar, Lectionary and Collects*

THEMES

Celebration is a central theme: the Te Deum sings of the saints' rejoicing and praise: we give thanks for the faithful followers of Christ; we celebrate together in company with others. Perhaps a more accessible word for children than celebration is 'fun', and one way of exploring this idea is the fun fair. Historically many of our fairs were held on or near a saint's day (Goose Fairs at Michaelmas; hiring fairs at Martinmas; Smithfield's Bartholomew Fair). These activities use bunting and the carousel to bring together the fun, variety and unity of All Saints: the carousel can also be used to teach about the cycle of the Christian year.

We all are saints, as St Paul frequently reminds us. The activity for the youngest children is based on the song 'I sing a song of the saints of God' and involves them dressing up, another fun activity.

TIMING

The bunting and carousel will each take one session.

Activity ideas
All Saints' bunting – for younger children

Talk about special occasions and how families decorate their homes for Christmas and for birthday parties to help them celebrate these special events. Then explain that All Saints' Tide is a major festival of the Church and so they are going to decorate the room with colourful bunting.

In Christian art saints are often shown with their special emblem or symbol. The emblem was often something which reminded viewers of the life of the saint, e.g. a set of keys for St Peter because Jesus said that he would be given the keys of heaven. The emblem was sometimes a reminder of how the saint died, e.g. the stones for St Stephen. The emblems therefore gave viewers a clue about who the person was. Talk about the emblems and saints listed below.

St Antony, 17 January – Tau cross

St Valentine, 14 February – the children could draw a heart

St Patrick, 17 March – red saltire

St Mark, 25 April – a winged lion

St Helena, 21 May – a gold cross on a purple field

St Peter, 29 June – a set of keys

St James, 25 July – a scallop shell

The Blessed Virgin Mary, 8 September – see chapter beginning on page 80

St Matthew, 21 September – an angel

St Luke, 18 October – a winged ox

St Hugh of Lincoln, 17 November – a swan

St Nicholas – 6 December – three gold roundels or balls

St Ambrose, 7 December – a beehive

St Stephen, 26 December – stones and a palm branch

St John the Evangelist, 27 December – a rising eagle

METHOD

- Give each child a flag and ask them to draw a picture of their favourite saint on one side of the flag and on the other that saint's symbol or emblem. They can make up a suitable emblem if they prefer.
- Attach the flags to a long piece of string with a stapler and hang up.

'I sing a song of the saints of God' – for younger children

Provide the group with a collection of dressing-up clothes or appropriate props so that they can act out this song, given in full on page 98.

You will need

pre-cut card flags in different colours for bunting

a long piece of string

stapler

colouring materials

pictures of saints with their symbols or special emblems

I sing a song of the saints of God

Lesbia Scott

'Grand Isle'
John Henry Hopkins

In sturdy march time

1. I sing a song of the saints of God, _____ Pa - tient and brave and
2. They loved their Lord so ___ dear, so dear, And ___ his love _ made them
3. They lived not on - ly in a - ges past, There are hun - dreds of thou - sands

true, Who _ toiled and _ fought and _ lived and died For the
strong; And they fol - lowed the right, for ___ Je - sus' sake, The __
still, The _ world is ___ bright with the joy - ous saints Who __

Lord they _ loved and knew. And _ one was a doc - tor, and
whole of their good lives long. And _ one was a sol - dier, and
love to do Je - sus' will. You can meet them in schools, or in

one was a queen, And _ one was a shep - herd-ess on the _ green: They were
one was a priest, And _ one was _ slain by a fierce wild _ beast: And there's
lanes or at sea, In ___ church or in trains, or in shops or at tea, For the

all of them saints of ___ God and I mean, God help - ing, to be one too.
not a - ny rea - son, _ no, not the least, Why I shouldn't be one too.
saints of___ God are just folk like _ me, And I mean to be one too.

An All Saints' carousel – for older children

From the information provided in the themes section explain how All Saints' Tide was a time of celebration for the Church. This carousel will remind them of the special celebrations around the Christian year.

METHOD

- Using the suggestions above ask the children to make small symbols for twelve saints from card. They can choose a saint for each of the twelve months of the year. If they are not sure what their chosen saint's symbol or emblem is they can make one up.
- Colour in these symbols and punch a hole in the top of each.
- Cover the bottle/tube and cheese box top and bottom with shiny paper.
- Attach equal lengths of gift ribbon to each of the saints' symbols and attach the hanging ribbon to the rim of the cheese box top with a stapler.
- Push the cork into the bottle top and balance the cheese box top on top of the cork so that the ribbons and symbols hang down.
- Carefully push the drawing pin through the top centre point of the cheese box and into the cork.
- Place the carousel on the cheese box bottom. It should now be able to spin around. If you do not have a small corked bottle use a cardboard tube and glue either end to the top and bottom of the cheese box. This version will not spin around but the teaching can remain the same.

You will need

a small empty corked bottle or card tube

top and bottom of a round cheese box

card

drawing materials

gift ribbon

scissors

drawing pin

decorative shiny paper

glue

hole punch

stapler

St Andrewstide

The Calling of Andrew *by Jane Gray. Pitminster Church, Somerset* Photo: *Peter Musgrave*

'Follow me, and I will make you fishers of men'. The non-inclusive language unfortunately persists, presumably because of the word play 'fishermen'/'fishers of men', but nothing could be more inclusive than the celebration of St Andrewstide. Andrew was a disciple of John the Baptist, when, with his brother Simon, he was the first to hear that calling of Jesus to which millions have since responded, 'Follow me'. That famous incident apart, very little is known about St Andrew. He is mentioned at the Feeding of the Five Thousand, at the episode in John's Gospel when some Greeks were asking to meet Jesus and finally in the Upper Room at Pentecost. Thereafter the information is even more scanty. The oldest sources connect him with Greece. His associations with the countries of which he is patron, Scotland and Russia, seem to have no foundation in fact. Nevertheless just those few gospel references justify the designation of St Andrewstide as a time for prayer and reflection on the worldwide mission of the Church. He was called by Jesus for the work of 'catching' men and women: the Five Thousand and the Greek inquirers suggest a mission beyond Israel and Judaism to a much wider field and the gift of the Holy Spirit is the one necessity for any who would go out and spread the word of God.

THEMES

It starts in a small insignificant locale: two fishermen on the lakeside; it ends in a faith that covers the globe, a gospel preached in thousands of languages, a Church containing a wealth of cultural diversity, yet serving and following the one Lord. We too may feel small and insignificant: yet God has a calling and a purpose for each of us, and in God's eyes we are no less – and no more – valued than were Andrew and his brother Simon. The fish badge for younger children reminds them that Christians are called to be '**Fishers of men**'. Jesus calls individuals: he calls every individual in the **whole world**. The most particular is the most universal: 'Follow me' is addressed to everyone, no-one is beyond the scope of God's love.

TIMING

The fish badge will take one session. The papier mâché globe will take two sessions to complete to allow it to dry.

Activity ideas
A fish badge – for younger children

The fish symbol was chosen by early Christians to represent Christ and was also sometimes used of the newly baptized and of the eucharist. The Greek word for fish – *ichthus* – also forms the acrostic in Greek *Iesous Christos Theou Uios Soter* – Jesus Christ, Son of God, Saviour. In early Christian art the fish symbol is often seen and it is still used by believers today as a Christian badge. The children can make their own *ichthus* badges to remind them that they too are fishers of men/women.

METHOD

- Cut out small lengths of string for each child.
- Help them to loop the string to make the *ichthus* shape.
- Glue the *ichthus* shape on to the card disc.
- An adult should then dry the glued shape with the aid of a hairdryer so that the children can colour their badges.
- Paint the badges and the string shape.
- An adult can dry the badges with the help of a hairdryer.
- Secure a safety pin with sticky tape on the back of each badge.

> **You will need**
> a disc of card for each child
> sticky tape
> safety pins
> PVA glue
> string
> scissors
> paints and paint brushes
> table coverings and aprons
> a hair dryer

A papier mâché globe – for older children

These papier mâché globes can provide a focus for prayer and discussion on the worldwide Church. If the group has a world mission link this could be incorporated. These globes can also be used as a visual aid while the children sing 'He's Got the Whole World in His Hands'.

METHOD

Session one

- Blow up the balloon so that it is globe-shaped and secure with a piece of string.
- In a bowl mix together two parts PVA glue with one part water.
- Tear the newspaper into small strips and paste on to the balloon.
- Paste five layers on to the balloon.
- Then paste on two layers of strips of the white toilet paper.
- Leave to dry for at least two days.

Session two

- Using an atlas for a guide the children can draw the continents on their papier mâché globes and paint in the sea. The string end is the top of the globe.
- They can then paint crosses on the globe to remind them that there are Christians on every continent of the globe.
- If there is time the children can also cut out pictures of people from different countries and stick these on the globe or label their continents with country names and flags.
- The globes can be hung up by the string and provide a focus for prayer.

You will need

a round balloon for each child

newspapers

bowl

white toilet paper

PVA glue diluted with water

spreaders

paints

string

an atlas

optional – magazines from mission societies, pictures of flags

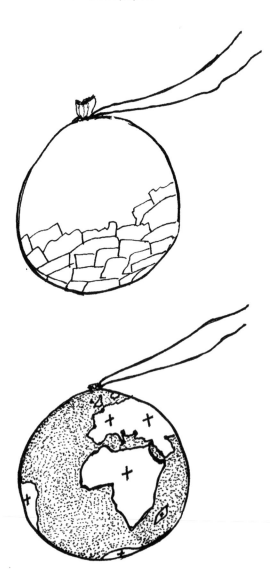

Appendix A

Church ....

Outings, activity days and residential consent form

for activities outside normal meeting times

Completed form to be taken on the trip by the group leader.

This section to be completed by the group leader

Note: Write name, nature, venue, dates and times in the section below. Give full details to parents/guardians on a separate sheet or in covering letter – name and nature of activity; venue/destination; date(s), times, place(s) of departure and return; cost and payment arrangements; transport arrangements; items needed (swimming kit, packed lunch, etc); emergency contact telephone numbers (e.g. residential centre, leader's mobile phone); date and person for reply.

Name of the group ....

Activity details (*see note above*) ....

....

Leader's name ....

1 Participant

Full name .... Date of birth ....

Address ....

....

....

Medical details

Doctor's name .... Phone ....

Surgery address ....

....

Participant's National Health number ....

Are there any problems with asthma? No/Yes ....

Are there any allergy problems? No/Yes ....

Are there are specific dietary needs? No/Yes ....

Will your child have any medicines
or tablets with them? No/Yes ....

Are there any other problems (eg diabetes, glandular fever, etc) which may affect normal activity?

No/Yes ....

2   **Emergency Contacts** (for duration of trip)

Name of parent/guardian ....

Daytime phone number ....

Evening phone number ....

First language of parent/guardian ....

Additional contact (e.g. grandparent/neighbour)

Name ....

Phone ....

First language of additional contact ....

---

3   **Consent**

I give permission for .... to attend
and take part in the activity/event detailed in this form.

In case of illness or accident I authorize

a)   the leader(s) of the event to sign on my behalf any written form
of consent required by the medical authorities should there be
any delay in them being able to contact me.

b)   the leader(s) to administer prescribed and non-prescribed
medication.

Signature of parent/guardian .... Date ....

Appendix B

Invitation for Good Friday event

Good Friday Workshop

Please come and join the .... Church Good Friday workshop.

There will be (*list of activities*)

        On: Friday ....
        Time: ....
        Place: ....

(*give details about refreshments*)

**Please ask your family and friends to join us for a service
at the end of the workshop at** .... (*give time*)

- -

To: (*name and telephone number of the coordinator of the event*)

From: ....

I will/will not be coming to the Good Friday workshop.

Signed: ....